JUST 1 POT

JUST **1** POT

Love Food ® is an imprint of
Parragon Books Ltd

Parragon
Queen Street House
4 Queen Street
Bath BA1 1HE, UK

Design: Terry Jeavons & Company

ISBN 978-1-4075-3386-5

Printed in China

This book uses metric and imperial
measurements. Follow the same units of
measurement throughout; do not mix metric
and imperial. All spoon measurements are
level, unless otherwise stated: teaspoons
are assumed to be 5 ml, and tablespoons
are assumed to be 15 ml. Unless otherwise
stated, milk is assumed to be full fat, eggs
and individual vegetables such as potatoes
are medium, and pepper is freshly ground
black pepper.

Recipes using raw or very lightly cooked eggs
should be avoided by children, the elderly,
pregnant women, convalescents, and anyone
suffering from an illness. Pregnant and
breast-feeding women are advised to avoid
eating peanuts and peanut products.

Contents

Introduction

If you love to cook but can't face the washing up, then *Just 1 Pot* is the book for you. As the name suggests, all the dishes can be cooked in a single pot, leaving you with very little to clean up and plenty of time to relax while the cooking takes care of itself.

As well as cutting down on washing up, one-pot cooking has so many other benefits.

- It's ideal for people with limited cooking space or equipment.
- It's a healthy way of cooking. You don't need to add a lot of fat and all the vitamins and minerals go into the cooking juices.
- You'll be saving energy by cooking on a single ring or burner.
- Most recipes are flexible and can be adjusted to the ingredients you have to hand.
- It's the ideal food for pot-luck suppers and feeding a crowd. One large pot is convenient to transport and the food can be served directly from it.

One-pot cooking doesn't limit you to soups and stews, although there are plenty of recipes for these in the book. In many parts of the world cooking in a single pot is the norm, whether it's in a frying pan or wok, or in a roasting tin or casserole dish. The wide choice of pots and pans opens up endless possibilities, allowing you to add all kinds of dishes and techniques to your one-pot repertoire. Spicy stir-fries and curries, fragrant rice and pasta dishes, gratins, bakes and braises are all easy to make in just one pot or pan.

You'll find chapters on meat and poultry, both of which develop marvellous flavours and succulent textures when cooked in a single pot. The section on fish includes classic soups and stews, as well as fish and rice combinations that can be cooked in a wide pan on the hob. Vegetables develop rich aromas and delectable textures from one-pot cooking too. The treatment works equally well for desserts – pies, crumbles and puddings can all be baked in a single dish and brought straight from the oven to the table.

With one-pot cooking it has never been easier to create delicious home-cooked meals with the minimum of fuss and effort, making it the ultimate in convenience for busy people. Just put the pot on the table and tuck in!

1 Meat

Long slow cooking in an enclosed pot is the ideal method for bringing out the best in cuts of meat that are too tough for frying or roasting. Enjoy the rich mellow flavours of pot-roast pork, or fruity Mediterranean lamb with apricots. Spice lovers will enjoy palate-tingling chilli con carne or a Caribbean-style pepper-pot stew. The moist heat encourages a magical exchange of flavours between meat, vegetables and seasonings, resulting in truly succulent and meltingly tender dishes.

Pot Roast with Potatoes & Dill

INGREDIENTS

serves 6

2½ tbsp plain flour

1 tsp salt

¼ tsp pepper

1 rolled brisket joint,
weighing 1.6 kg/3 lb 8 oz

2 tbsp vegetable oil

2 tbsp butter

1 onion, finely chopped

2 celery sticks, diced

2 carrots, peeled and diced

1 tsp dill seed

1 tsp dried thyme or oregano

350 ml/12 fl oz red wine

150–225 ml/5–8 fl oz beef
stock

4–5 potatoes, cut into large
chunks and boiled until just
tender

2 tbsp chopped fresh dill,
to serve

1 Preheat the oven to 140°C/275°F/Gas Mark 1. Mix 2 tablespoons of the flour with the salt and pepper in a shallow dish. Dip the meat to coat. Heat the oil in a flameproof casserole and brown the meat all over. Transfer to a plate. Add half the butter to the casserole and cook the onion, celery, carrots, dill seed and thyme for 5 minutes. Return the meat and juices to the casserole.

2 Pour in the wine and enough stock to reach one third of the way up the meat. Bring to the boil, cover and cook in the oven for 3 hours, turning the meat every 30 minutes. After it has been cooking for 2 hours, add the potatoes and more stock if necessary.

3 When ready, transfer the meat and vegetables to a warmed serving dish. Strain the cooking liquid to remove any solids, then return the liquid to the casserole.

4 Mix the remaining butter and flour to a paste. Bring the cooking liquid to the boil. Whisk in small pieces of the flour and butter paste, whisking constantly until the sauce is smooth. Pour the sauce over the meat and vegetables. Sprinkle with the fresh dill to serve.

Beef in Beer with Herb Dumplings

INGREDIENTS

serves 6

2 tbsp sunflower oil

2 large onions, thinly sliced

8 carrots, sliced

4 tbsp plain flour

1.25 kg/2 lb 12 oz stewing steak, cut into cubes

425 ml/15 fl oz stout

2 tsp muscovado sugar

2 bay leaves

1 tbsp chopped fresh thyme

salt and pepper

HERB DUMPLINGS

115 g/4 oz self-raising flour

pinch of salt

55 g/2 oz shredded suet

2 tbsp chopped fresh parsley, plus extra to garnish

about 4 tbsp water

1 Preheat the oven to 160°C/325°F/Gas Mark 3. Heat the oil in a flameproof casserole. Add the onions and carrots and cook over a low heat, stirring occasionally, for 5 minutes, or until the onions are soft. Meanwhile, place the flour in a polythene bag and season with salt and pepper. Add the stewing steak to the bag, tie the top and shake well to coat. Do this in batches, if necessary.

2 Remove the vegetables from the casserole with a slotted spoon and reserve. Add the stewing steak to the casserole, in batches, and cook, stirring frequently, until browned all over. Return all the meat and the onions and carrots to the casserole and sprinkle in any remaining seasoned flour. Pour in the stout and add the sugar, bay leaves and thyme. Bring to the boil, cover and transfer to the preheated oven to bake for 1¾ hours.

3 To make the herb dumplings, sift the flour and salt into a bowl.

4 Stir in the suet and parsley and add enough of the water to make a soft dough. Shape into small balls between the palms of your hands. Add to the casserole and return to the oven for 30 minutes. Remove and discard the bay leaves. Serve immediately, sprinkled with chopped parsley.

Daube of Beef

INGREDIENTS

serves 6

350 ml/12 fl oz dry white wine

2 tbsp brandy

1 tbsp white wine vinegar

4 shallots, sliced

4 carrots, sliced

1 garlic clove, finely chopped

6 black peppercorns

4 fresh thyme sprigs

1 fresh rosemary sprig

2 fresh parsley sprigs, plus extra to garnish

1 bay leaf

750 g/1 lb 10 oz beef topside, cut into 2.5-cm/1-inch cubes

2 tbsp olive oil

800 g/1 lb 12 oz canned chopped tomatoes

225 g/8 oz mushrooms, sliced

strip of finely pared orange rind

55 g/2 oz Bayonne ham, cut into strips

12 black olives

salt

1 Combine the wine, brandy, vinegar, shallots, carrots, garlic, peppercorns, thyme, rosemary, parsley and bay leaf, and season to taste with salt. Add the beef, stirring to coat, then cover with clingfilm and leave in the refrigerator to marinate for 8 hours, or overnight.

2 Preheat the oven to 150°C/300°F/Gas Mark 2. Drain the beef, reserving the marinade, and pat dry on kitchen paper. Heat half the oil in a large, flameproof casserole. Add the beef in batches and cook over a medium heat, stirring, for 3–4 minutes, or until browned. Transfer the beef to a plate with a slotted spoon. Brown the remaining beef, adding more oil, if necessary.

3 Return all of the beef to the casserole and add the tomatoes and their juices, mushrooms and orange rind. Strain the reserved marinade into the casserole. Bring to the boil, cover and cook in the oven for 2½ hours.

4 Remove the casserole from the oven, add the ham and olives and return it to the oven to cook for a further 30 minutes, or until the beef is very tender. Discard the orange rind and serve straight from the casserole, garnished with parsley.

Beef Goulash

INGREDIENTS

serves 4

2 tbsp vegetable oil

1 large onion, chopped

1 garlic clove, crushed

750 g/1 lb 10 oz lean stewing steak

2 tbsp paprika

425 g/15 oz canned chopped tomatoes

2 tbsp tomato purée

1 large red pepper, deseeded and chopped

175 g/6 oz mushrooms, sliced

600 ml/1 pint beef stock

1 tbsp cornflour

1 tbsp water

4 tbsp natural yogurt

paprika, for sprinkling

salt and pepper

chopped fresh parsley, to garnish

freshly cooked long-grain rice and wild rice, to serve

1 Heat the vegetable oil in a large frying pan and cook the onion and garlic for 3–4 minutes.

2 Cut the stewing steak into chunks and cook over a high heat for 3 minutes until browned all over. Add the paprika and stir well, then add the chopped tomatoes, tomato purée, red pepper and mushrooms. Cook for 2 minutes, stirring frequently.

3 Pour in the beef stock. Bring to the boil, then reduce the heat. Cover and simmer for 1½–2 hours until the meat is tender.

4 Blend the cornflour with the water, then add to the pan, stirring until thickened and smooth. Cook for 1 minute, then season to taste with salt and pepper.

5 Put the natural yogurt in a serving bowl and sprinkle with a little paprika.

6 Transfer the beef goulash to a warmed serving dish, garnish with chopped fresh parsley and serve with rice and yogurt.

Chilli con Carne

INGREDIENTS

serves **4**

750 g/1 lb 10 oz lean stewing
steak

2 tbsp vegetable oil

1 large onion, sliced

2–4 garlic cloves, crushed

1 tbsp plain flour

425 ml/15 fl oz tomato juice

400 g/14 oz canned tomatoes

1–2 tbsp sweet chilli sauce

1 tsp ground cumin

425 g/15 oz canned red
kidney beans, drained and
rinsed

½ teaspoon dried oregano

1–2 tbsp chopped fresh
parsley

salt and pepper

sprigs of fresh herbs,
to garnish

freshly cooked rice and
tortillas, to serve

1 Preheat the oven to 160°C/325°F/Gas Mark 3.
Using a sharp knife, cut the beef into 2-cm/¾-
inch cubes. Heat the vegetable oil in a large
flameproof casserole dish and fry the beef over
a medium heat until well sealed on all sides.
Remove the beef from the casserole with a
slotted spoon and reserve until required.

2 Add the onion and garlic to the casserole
and fry until lightly browned; then stir in the
flour and cook for 1–2 minutes.

3 Stir in the tomato juice and tomatoes and
bring to the boil. Return the beef to the
casserole and add the chilli sauce, cumin and
salt and pepper to taste. Cover and cook in the
preheated oven for 1½ hours, or until the beef
is almost tender.

4 Stir in the kidney beans, oregano and
parsley, and adjust the seasoning to taste, if
necessary. Cover the casserole and return to
the oven for 45 minutes. Transfer to 4 large,
warmed serving plates, garnish with sprigs of
fresh herbs and serve immediately with freshly
cooked rice and tortillas.

Beef & Vegetable Stew with Corn

INGREDIENTS

serves **4**

450 g/1 lb braising steak

1½ tbsp plain flour

1 tsp hot paprika

1–1½ tsp chilli powder

1 tsp ground ginger

2 tbsp olive oil

1 large onion, cut into chunks

3 garlic cloves, sliced

2 celery sticks, sliced

225 g/8 oz carrots, chopped

300 ml/10 fl oz lager

300 ml/10 fl oz beef stock

350 g/12 oz potatoes, chopped

1 red pepper, deseeded and chopped

2 corn on the cob, halved

115 g/4 oz tomatoes, quartered

115 g/4 oz shelled fresh or frozen peas

1 tbsp chopped fresh coriander

salt and pepper

1 Trim any fat or gristle from the beef and cut into 2.5-cm/1-inch chunks. Mix the flour and spices together. Toss the beef in the spiced flour until well coated.

2 Heat the oil in a large, heavy-based saucepan and cook the onion, garlic and celery, stirring frequently, for 5 minutes, or until soft. Add the beef and cook over a high heat, stirring frequently, for 3 minutes, or until browned on all sides and sealed.

3 Add the carrots, then remove from the heat. Gradually stir in the lager and stock, then return to the heat and bring to the boil, stirring. Reduce the heat, cover and simmer, stirring occasionally, for 1½ hours.

4 Add the potatoes to the saucepan and simmer for a further 15 minutes. Add the red pepper and corn on the cob and simmer for a further 15 minutes, then add the tomatoes and peas and simmer for a further 10 minutes, or until the beef and vegetables are tender. Season to taste with salt and pepper, stir in the coriander and serve.

Beef Stroganoff

INGREDIENTS

serves 4

15 g/½ oz dried ceps

350 g/12 oz beef fillet

2 tbsp olive oil

115 g/4 oz shallots, sliced

175 g/6 oz chestnut mushrooms

½ tsp Dijon mustard

5 tbsp double cream

salt and pepper

freshly cooked pasta, to serve

fresh chives, to garnish

1 Place the dried ceps in a bowl and cover with hot water. Leave to soak for 20 minutes. Meanwhile, cut the beef against the grain into 5-mm/¼-inch thick slices, then into 1-cm/½-inch long strips, and reserve.

2 Drain the mushrooms, reserving the soaking liquid, and chop. Strain the soaking liquid through a fine-mesh sieve or coffee filter and reserve.

3 Heat half the oil in a large frying pan. Add the shallots and cook over a low heat, stirring occasionally, for 5 minutes, or until soft. Add the soaked mushrooms, reserved soaking water and whole chestnut mushrooms and cook, stirring frequently, for 10 minutes, or until almost all of the liquid has evaporated, then transfer the mixture to a plate.

4 Heat the remaining oil in the pan, add the beef and cook, stirring frequently, for 4 minutes, or until browned all over. You may need to do this in batches. Return the mushroom mixture to the pan and season to taste with salt and pepper. Place the mustard and cream in a small bowl and stir to mix, then fold into the meat and mushroom mixture. Heat through gently, then serve with freshly cooked pasta, garnished with chives.

Pepper Pot-Style Stew

INGREDIENTS

serves ❹

450 g/1 lb braising steak

1½ tbsp plain flour

2 tbsp olive oil

1 Spanish onion, chopped

3–4 garlic cloves, crushed

1 fresh green chilli, deseeded and chopped

3 celery sticks, sliced

4 whole cloves

1 tsp ground allspice

1–2 teaspoons hot pepper sauce, or to taste

600 ml/1 pint beef stock

225 g/8 oz deseeded and peeled squash, such as acorn, cut into small chunks

1 large red pepper, deseeded and chopped

4 tomatoes, roughly chopped

115 g/4 oz okra, trimmed and halved

mixed wild rice and basmati rice, to serve

1 Trim any fat or gristle from the beef and cut into 2.5-cm/1-inch chunks. Toss the beef in the flour until well coated and reserve any remaining flour.

2 Heat the oil in a large, heavy-based saucepan and cook the onion, garlic, chilli and celery with the cloves and allspice, stirring frequently, for 5 minutes, or until soft. Add the beef and cook over a high heat, stirring frequently, for 3 minutes, or until browned on all sides and sealed. Sprinkle in the reserved flour and cook, stirring constantly, for 2 minutes, then remove from the heat.

3 Add the hot pepper sauce and gradually stir in the stock, then return to the heat and bring to the boil, stirring. Reduce the heat, cover and simmer, stirring occasionally, for 1½ hours.

4 Add the squash and red pepper to the pan and simmer for a further 15 minutes. Add the tomatoes and okra and simmer for a further 15 minutes, or until the beef is tender. Serve with mixed wild and basmati rice.

Osso Bucco

INGREDIENTS

serves 4

1 tbsp virgin olive oil

4 tbsp butter

2 onions, chopped

1 leek, sliced

3 tbsp plain flour

4 thick slices of veal shin
(osso bucco)

300 ml/½ pint white wine

300 ml/½ pint veal or
chicken stock

salt and pepper

GREMOLATA

2 tbsp chopped fresh
parsley

1 garlic clove, finely
chopped

grated rind of 1 lemon

1 Heat the oil and butter in a large, heavy-based frying pan. Add the onions and leek and cook over a low heat, stirring occasionally, for 5 minutes, until softened.

2 Spread out the flour on a plate and season with salt and pepper. Toss the pieces of veal in the flour to coat, shaking off any excess. Add the veal to the pan, increase the heat to high and cook until browned on both sides.

3 Gradually stir in the wine and stock and bring just to the boil, stirring constantly. Reduce the heat, cover and simmer for 1¼ hours, or until the veal is very tender.

4 Meanwhile, make the gremolata by mixing the parsley, garlic and lemon rind in a small bowl.

5 Transfer the veal to a warmed serving dish with a slotted spoon. Bring the sauce to the boil and cook, stirring occasionally, until thickened and reduced. Pour the sauce over the veal, sprinkle with the gremolata and serve immediately.

1

Irish Stew

INGREDIENTS

serves 4

4 tbsp plain flour

1.3 kg/3 lb middle neck of lamb, trimmed of visible fat

3 large onions, chopped

3 carrots, sliced

450 g/1 lb potatoes, quartered

½ tsp dried thyme

850 ml/1½ pints hot beef stock

2 tbsp chopped fresh parsley, to garnish

salt and pepper

1 Preheat the oven to 160°C/325°F/Gas Mark 3. Spread the flour on a plate and season with salt and pepper. Roll the pieces of lamb in the flour to coat, shaking off any excess, and arrange in the base of a casserole.

2 Layer the onions, carrots and potatoes on top of the lamb.

3 Sprinkle in the thyme and pour in the stock, then cover and cook in the preheated oven for 2½ hours. Garnish with the chopped fresh parsley and serve straight from the casserole.

Lamb Stew with Chickpeas

INGREDIENTS

serves **4**–**6**

6 tbsp olive oil

225 g/8 oz chorizo sausage, cut into 5-mm/¼-inch thick slices, casings removed

2 large onions, chopped

6 large garlic cloves, crushed

900 g/2 lb boned leg of lamb, cut into 5-cm/2-inch chunks

250 ml/9 fl oz lamb stock or water

125 ml/4 fl oz red wine, such as Rioja or Tempranillo

2 tbsp sherry vinegar

800 g/1 lb 12 oz canned chopped tomatoes

4 sprigs fresh thyme, plus extra to garnish

2 bay leaves

½ tsp sweet Spanish paprika

800 g/1 lb 12 oz canned chickpeas, rinsed and drained

salt and pepper

1 Heat 4 tablespoons of the oil in a large, heavy-based flameproof casserole over a medium–high heat. Reduce the heat, add the chorizo and fry for 1 minute. Transfer to a plate. Add the onions to the casserole and fry for 2 minutes, then add the garlic and continue frying for 3 minutes, or until the onions are soft, but not brown. Remove from the casserole and set aside.

2 Heat the remaining 2 tablespoons of oil in the casserole. Add the lamb cubes in a single layer without over-crowding the casserole, and fry until browned on each side; work in batches, if necessary.

3 Return the onion mixture and chorizo to the casserole with all the lamb. Stir in the stock, wine, vinegar, tomatoes with their juices and salt and pepper to taste. Bring to the boil, scraping any glazed bits from the base of the casserole. Reduce the heat and stir in the thyme, bay leaves and paprika.

4 Transfer to a preheated oven, 160°C/325°F/ Gas Mark 3, and cook, covered, for 40–45 minutes until the lamb is tender. Stir in the chickpeas and return to the oven, uncovered, for 10 minutes, or until they are heated through and the juices are reduced.

5 Taste and adjust the seasoning. Serve garnished with thyme.

Mediterranean Lamb with Apricots & Pistachio Nuts

INGREDIENTS

pinch of saffron threads

2 tbsp almost-boiling water

450 g/1 lb lean, boneless lamb, such as leg steaks

1½ tbsp plain flour

1 tsp ground coriander

½ tsp ground cumin

½ tsp ground allspice

1 tbsp olive oil

1 onion, chopped

2–3 garlic cloves, chopped

450 ml/16 fl oz lamb or chicken stock

1 cinnamon stick, bruised

85 g/3 oz dried apricots, roughly chopped

175 g/6 oz courgettes, sliced

115 g/4 oz cherry tomatoes

1 tbsp chopped fresh coriander

salt and pepper

2 tbsp roughly chopped pistachio nuts, to garnish

couscous, to serve

serves ❹

1 Put the saffron threads in a heatproof jug with the water and leave for at least 10 minutes to infuse. Trim off any fat or gristle from the lamb and cut into 2.5-cm/1-inch chunks. Mix the flour and spices together, then toss the lamb in the spiced flour until well coated and reserve any remaining spiced flour.

2 Heat the oil in a large, heavy-based saucepan and cook the onion and garlic, stirring frequently, for 5 minutes, or until soft. Add the lamb and cook over a high heat, stirring frequently, for 3 minutes, or until browned on all sides and sealed. Sprinkle in the reserved spiced flour and cook, stirring constantly, for 2 minutes, then remove from the heat.

3 Gradually stir in the stock with the saffron and its soaking liquid, then return to the heat and bring to the boil, stirring. Add the cinnamon stick and apricots. Reduce the heat, cover and simmer, stirring occasionally, for 1 hour.

4 Add the courgettes and tomatoes and cook for a further 15 minutes. Discard the cinnamon stick. Stir in the fresh coriander and season to taste with salt and pepper. Serve sprinkled with the pistachio nuts, accompanied by couscous.

Lamb with Pears

INGREDIENTS

serves 4

1 tbsp olive oil

1 kg/2 lb 4 oz best end-of-neck lamb cutlets, trimmed of visible fat

6 pears, peeled, cored and quartered

1 tsp ground ginger

4 potatoes, diced

4 tbsp dry cider

450 g/1 lb green beans

salt and pepper

2 tbsp snipped fresh chives, to garnish

1 Preheat the oven to 160°C/325°F/Gas Mark 3. Heat the olive oil in a flameproof casserole over a medium heat. Add the lamb and cook, turning frequently, for 5–10 minutes, or until browned on all sides.

2 Arrange the pear quarters on top, then sprinkle over the ginger. Cover with the potatoes. Pour in the cider and season to taste with salt and pepper. Cover and cook in the preheated oven for 1¼ hours.

3 Trim the stalk ends of the green beans. Remove the casserole from the oven and add the beans, then re-cover and return to the oven for a further 30 minutes. Taste and adjust the seasoning. Sprinkle with the chives and serve.

Pot-Roast Pork

INGREDIENTS

serves 4

1 tbsp sunflower oil

55 g/2 oz butter

1 kg/2 lb 4 oz boned and rolled pork loin joint

4 shallots, chopped

6 juniper berries

2 fresh thyme sprigs, plus extra to garnish

150 ml/5 fl oz dry cider

150 ml/5 fl oz chicken stock or water

8 celery sticks, chopped

2 tbsp plain flour

150 ml/5 fl oz double cream

salt and pepper

freshly cooked peas, to serve

1 Heat the oil with half the butter in a heavy-based saucepan or flameproof casserole. Add the pork and cook over a medium heat, turning frequently, for 5–10 minutes, or until browned. Transfer to a plate.

2 Add the shallots to the pan and cook, stirring frequently, for 5 minutes, or until soft. Add the juniper berries and thyme sprigs and return the pork to the pan, with any juices that have collected on the plate. Pour in the cider and stock, season to taste with salt and pepper, then cover and simmer for 30 minutes. Turn the pork over and add the celery. Re-cover the pan and cook for a further 40 minutes.

3 Meanwhile, make a beurre manié by mashing the remaining butter with the flour in a small bowl. Transfer the pork and celery to a platter with a slotted spoon and keep warm. Remove and discard the juniper berries and thyme. Whisk the beurre manié, a little at a time, into the simmering cooking liquid. Cook, stirring constantly, for 2 minutes, then stir in the cream and bring to the boil.

4 Slice the pork and spoon a little of the sauce over it. Garnish with thyme sprigs and serve immediately with the celery, peas and remaining sauce.

1

Pork with Red Cabbage

INGREDIENTS

1 tbsp sunflower oil

750 g/1 lb 10 oz boned and rolled pork loin joint

1 onion, finely chopped

500 g/1 lb 2 oz red cabbage, thick stems removed and leaves shredded

2 large cooking apples, peeled, cored and sliced

3 cloves

1 tsp brown sugar

3 tbsp lemon juice, and a thinly pared strip of lemon rind

lemon wedges, to garnish

serves ❹

1 Preheat the oven to 160°C/325°F/Gas Mark 3. Heat the oil in a flameproof casserole. Add the pork and cook over a medium heat, turning frequently, for 5–10 minutes, or until browned. Transfer to a plate.

2 Add the chopped onion to the casserole and cook over a low heat, stirring occasionally, for 5 minutes, or until softened. Add the cabbage, in batches, and cook, stirring, for 2 minutes. Transfer each batch (mixed with some onion) into a bowl with a slotted spoon.

3 Add the apple slices, cloves and sugar to the bowl and mix well, then place about half the mixture in the base of the casserole. Top with the pork and add the remaining cabbage mixture. Sprinkle in the lemon juice and add the strip of rind. Cover and cook in the preheated oven for 1½ hours.

4 Transfer the pork to a plate. Transfer the cabbage mixture to the plate with a slotted spoon and keep warm. Bring the cooking juices to the boil over a high heat and reduce slightly.

5 Slice the pork and arrange on warmed serving plates, surrounded with the cabbage mixture. Spoon the cooking juices over the meat and serve with wedges of lemon.

Rice & Peas

INGREDIENTS

serves 4

1 tbsp olive oil

4 tbsp butter

55 g/2 oz pancetta or streaky bacon, chopped

1 small onion, chopped

1.4 litres/2½ pints hot chicken stock

200 g/7 oz risotto rice

3 tbsp chopped fresh parsley

225 g/8 oz fresh, frozen or canned petits pois

55 g/2 oz Parmesan cheese, grated

pepper

1 Heat the olive oil and half of the butter in a heavy-based pan. Add the pancetta and onion and cook over a low heat, stirring occasionally, for 5 minutes until the onion is soft and translucent, but not brown.

2 Add the stock and fresh peas, if using, to the pan and bring to the boil. Stir in the rice and season to taste with pepper. Bring to the boil, reduce the heat and simmer, stirring occasionally, for 20–30 minutes until the rice is tender.

3 Add the parsley and frozen or canned petits pois, if using these instead of fresh peas, and cook for about 8 minutes until the peas are heated through. Stir in the remaining butter and the Parmesan cheese.

4 Transfer to a warmed serving dish and serve immediately with pepper.

Potato & Sausage Pan-Fry

INGREDIENTS

675 g/1 lb 8 oz waxy potatoes, cubed

25 g/1 oz butter

8 large herb sausages

4 smoked bacon rashers

1 onion, quartered

1 courgette, sliced

150 ml/¼ pint dry white wine

300 ml/½ pint vegetable stock

1 tsp Worcestershire sauce

2 tbsp chopped mixed fresh herbs

salt and pepper

chopped fresh herbs, to garnish

serves 4

1 Bring a large saucepan of lightly salted water to the boil, add the cubed potatoes and cook for 10 minutes, or until soft. Drain thoroughly and set aside.

2 Meanwhile, melt the butter in a large frying pan. Add the herb sausages and cook for 5 minutes, turning them frequently to ensure that they brown evenly on all sides.

3 Add the bacon rashers, onion, courgette and potatoes to the pan. Cook for a further 10 minutes, stirring, and turning the sausages frequently.

4 Stir in the white wine, stock, Worcestershire sauce and chopped mixed herbs. Season to taste with salt and pepper and cook the mixture over a gentle heat for 10 minutes. Add more salt and pepper, if necessary.

5 Transfer the potato and sausage pan-fry to warmed serving plates, garnish with chopped fresh herbs and serve at once.

2 Poultry

Versatile chicken forms the basis of a
wealth of one-pot meals – from the classic
coq au vin to spicy curries. Turkey takes on
a new lease of life in a speedy one-pan stir-
fry with cranberries, or try it Mexican-style
with chillies. Sweet and meaty duck goes
into a fragrant one-pot Asian braise, or a
sweet-sharp Mediterranean-style stew
with olives. The possibilities are endless –
all you need is a pot.

Chicken & Barley Stew

INGREDIENTS

serves 4

2 tbsp vegetable oil

8 small, skinless chicken thighs

500 ml/18 fl oz chicken stock

100 g/3½ oz pearl barley, rinsed and drained

200 g/7 oz small new potatoes, scrubbed and halved lengthways

2 large carrots, peeled and sliced

1 leek, trimmed and sliced

2 shallots, sliced

1 tbsp tomato purée

1 bay leaf

1 courgette, trimmed and sliced

2 tbsp chopped fresh flat-leaf parsley, plus extra sprigs to garnish

2 tbsp plain flour

salt and pepper

fresh crusty bread, to serve

1 Heat the oil in a large saucepan over a medium heat. Add the chicken and cook for 3 minutes, then turn over and cook on the other side for a further 2 minutes. Add the stock, barley, potatoes, carrots, leek, shallots, tomato purée and bay leaf. Bring to the boil, reduce the heat and simmer for 30 minutes.

2 Add the courgette and chopped parsley, cover the pan and cook for a further 20 minutes, or until the chicken is cooked through. Remove the bay leaf and discard.

3 In a separate bowl, mix the flour with 4 tablespoons of water and stir into a smooth paste. Add it to the stew and cook, stirring, over a low heat for a further 5 minutes. Season to taste with salt and pepper.

4 Remove from the heat, ladle into individual serving bowls and garnish with sprigs of fresh parsley. Serve with fresh crusty bread.

Coq au Vin

INGREDIENTS

serves **4**

55 g/2 oz butter

2 tbsp olive oil

1.8 kg/4 lb chicken pieces

115 g/4 oz rindless smoked bacon, cut into strips

115 g/4 oz baby onions

115 g/4 oz chestnut mushrooms, halved

2 garlic cloves, finely chopped

2 tbsp brandy

225 ml/8 fl oz red wine

300 ml/10 fl oz chicken stock

1 bouquet garni

2 tbsp plain flour

salt and pepper

bay leaves, to garnish

1 Melt half the butter with the olive oil in a large, flameproof casserole. Add the chicken and cook over a medium heat, stirring, for 8–10 minutes, or until golden brown all over. Add the bacon, onions, mushrooms and garlic.

2 Pour in the brandy and set it alight with a match or taper. When the flames have died down, add the wine, stock and bouquet garni and season to taste with salt and pepper. Bring to the boil, reduce the heat and simmer gently for 1 hour, or until the chicken pieces are cooked through and tender. Meanwhile, make a beurre manié by mashing the remaining butter with the flour in a small bowl.

3 Remove and discard the bouquet garni. Transfer the chicken to a large plate and keep warm. Stir the beurre manié into the casserole, a little at a time. Bring to the boil, return the chicken to the casserole and serve immediately, garnished with bay leaves.

Italian-Style Roast Chicken

INGREDIENTS

serves 6

2.5 kg/5 lb 8 oz chicken

fresh rosemary sprigs

175 g/6 oz feta cheese, coarsely grated

2 tbsp sun-dried tomato purée

60 g/2 oz butter, softened

1 bulb garlic

1 kg/2 lb 4 oz new potatoes, halved if large

1 each red, green and yellow pepper, deseeded and cut into chunks

3 courgettes, thinly sliced

2 tbsp olive oil

salt and pepper

600 ml/1 pint ready-made gravy, to serve

1 Preheat the oven to 190°C/375°F/Gas Mark 5. Rinse the chicken inside and out with cold water and drain well. Carefully cut between the skin and the top of the breast meat using a small pointed knife. Slide a finger into the slit and carefully enlarge it to form a pocket. Continue until the skin is completely lifted away from both breasts and the top of the legs.

2 Chop the leaves from 3 rosemary stems. Mix with the feta cheese, sun-dried tomato purée, butter, and pepper to taste, then spoon under the skin. Put the chicken in a large roasting tin, cover with foil and cook in the preheated oven, for 20 minutes per 500 g/ 1 lb 2 oz, plus 20 minutes.

3 Break the garlic bulb into cloves but do not peel. Add the vegetables and garlic to the chicken after 40 minutes.

4 Drizzle with oil, tuck in a few stems of rosemary and season with salt and pepper. Cook for the remaining calculated time, removing the foil for the last 40 minutes to brown the chicken. Serve immediately with the vegetables and gravy.

Spicy Aromatic Chicken

INGREDIENTS

4–8 chicken pieces, skinned

½ lemon, cut into wedges

4 tbsp olive oil

1 onion, roughly chopped

2 large garlic cloves, finely chopped

125 ml/4 fl oz dry white wine

400 g/14 oz canned chopped tomatoes in juice

pinch of sugar

½ tsp ground cinnamon

½ tsp ground cloves

½ tsp ground allspice

400g/14 oz canned artichoke hearts or okra, drained

8 black olives, stoned

salt and pepper

serves ❹

1 Rub the chicken pieces with the lemon. Heat the oil in a large flameproof casserole or lidded frying pan. Add the onion and garlic and fry for 5 minutes, until softened. Add the chicken pieces and fry for 5–10 minutes, until browned on all sides.

2 Pour in the wine and add the tomatoes with their can juices, the sugar, cinnamon, cloves, allspice, salt and pepper and bring to the boil. Cover the casserole and simmer for 45 minutes–1 hour, until the chicken is tender.

3 Meanwhile, if using artichoke hearts, cut them in half. Add with the olives to the casserole 10 minutes before the end of cooking, and continue to simmer until heated through. Serve hot.

Chicken in White Wine

INGREDIENTS

serves 4

55 g/2 oz butter

2 tbsp olive oil

2 rindless, thick streaky bacon rashers, chopped

115 g/4 oz baby onions, peeled

1 garlic clove, finely chopped

1.8 kg/4 lb chicken pieces

400 ml/14 fl oz dry white wine

300 ml/10 fl oz chicken stock

1 bouquet garni

115 g/4 oz button mushrooms

25 g/1 oz plain flour

salt and pepper

fresh mixed herbs, to garnish

1 Preheat the oven to 160°C/325°F/Gas Mark 3. Melt half the butter with the oil in a flameproof casserole. Add the bacon and cook over a medium heat, stirring, for 5–10 minutes, or until golden brown. Transfer the bacon to a large plate. Add the onions and garlic to the casserole and cook over a low heat, stirring occasionally, for 10 minutes, or until golden. Transfer to the plate. Add the chicken and cook over a medium heat, stirring constantly, for 8–10 minutes, or until golden. Transfer to the plate.

2 Drain off any excess fat from the casserole. Stir in the wine and stock and bring to the boil, scraping any sediment off the base. Add the bouquet garni and season to taste. Return the bacon, onions and chicken to the casserole. Cover and cook in the preheated oven for 1 hour. Add the mushrooms, re-cover and cook for 15 minutes. Meanwhile, make a beurre manié by mashing the remaining butter with the flour in a small bowl.

3 Remove the casserole from the oven and set over a medium heat. Remove and discard the bouquet garni. Whisk in the beurre manié, a little at a time. Bring to the boil, stirring constantly, then serve, garnished with fresh herb sprigs.

Florida Chicken

INGREDIENTS

serves 4

450 g/1 lb skinless, boneless chicken

1½ tbsp plain flour

1 tbsp olive oil

1 onion, cut into wedges

2 celery sticks, sliced

150 ml/5 fl oz orange juice

300 ml/10 fl oz chicken stock

1 tbsp light soy sauce

1–2 tsp clear honey

1 tbsp grated orange rind

1 orange pepper, deseeded and chopped

225 g/8 oz courgettes, sliced into half moons

2 small corn on the cob, halved, or 100 g/3½ oz baby sweetcorn

1 orange, peeled and segmented

salt and pepper

1 tbsp chopped fresh parsley, to garnish

1 Lightly rinse the chicken and pat dry with kitchen paper. Cut into bite-sized pieces. Season the flour well with salt and pepper. Toss the chicken in the seasoned flour until well coated and reserve any remaining seasoned flour.

2 Heat the oil in a large, heavy-based frying pan and cook the chicken over a high heat, stirring frequently, for 5 minutes, or until golden on all sides and sealed. Using a slotted spoon, transfer the chicken to a plate.

3 Add the onion and celery to the pan and cook over a medium heat, stirring frequently, for 5 minutes, or until soft. Sprinkle in the reserved seasoned flour and cook, stirring constantly, for 2 minutes, then remove from the heat. Gradually stir in the orange juice, stock, soy sauce and honey, followed by the orange rind, then return to the heat and bring to the boil, stirring.

4 Return the chicken to the pan. Reduce the heat, cover and simmer, stirring occasionally, for 15 minutes. Add the orange pepper, courgettes and corn on the cob and simmer for a further 10 minutes, or until the chicken and vegetables are tender. Add the orange segments, stir well and heat through for 1 minute. Serve garnished with the parsley.

Thai Green Chicken Curry

INGREDIENTS

serves 4

2 tbsp groundnut or
sunflower oil

2 tbsp ready-made green
curry paste

500 g/1 lb 2 oz skinless
boneless chicken breasts,
cut into cubes

2 kaffir lime leaves, roughly
torn

1 lemon grass stalk, finely
chopped

225 ml/8 fl oz canned
coconut milk

16 baby aubergines, halved

2 tbsp Thai fish sauce

fresh Thai basil sprigs,
to garnish

kaffir lime leaves, thinly
sliced, to garnish

1 Heat the oil in a preheated wok or large, heavy-based frying pan. Add the curry paste and stir-fry briefly until all the aromas are released.

2 Add the chicken, lime leaves and lemon grass and stir-fry for 3–4 minutes, until the meat is beginning to colour. Add the coconut milk and aubergines and simmer gently for 8–10 minutes, or until tender.

3 Stir in the fish sauce and serve immediately, garnished with Thai basil sprigs and lime leaves.

Chicken Jalfrezi

INGREDIENTS

serves ❹

½ tsp cumin seeds

½ tsp coriander seeds

1 tsp mustard oil

3 tbsp vegetable oil

1 large onion, finely chopped

3 garlic cloves, crushed

1 tbsp tomato purée

2 tomatoes, peeled and chopped

1 tsp ground turmeric

½ tsp chilli powder

½ tsp garam masala

1 tsp red wine vinegar

1 small red pepper, deseeded and chopped

125 g/4½ oz frozen broad beans

500 g/1 lb 2 oz cooked chicken, chopped

salt

fresh coriander sprigs, to garnish

freshly cooked rice, to serve

1 Grind the cumin and coriander seeds in a mortar with a pestle, then reserve. Heat the mustard oil in a large, heavy-based frying pan over a high heat for 1 minute, or until it begins to smoke. Add the vegetable oil, reduce the heat and add the onion and garlic. Cook for 10 minutes, or until golden.

2 Add the tomato purée, chopped tomatoes, turmeric, ground cumin and coriander seeds, chilli powder, garam masala and vinegar to the pan. Stir the mixture until fragrant.

3 Add the red pepper and broad beans and stir for a further 2 minutes, or until the pepper is softened. Stir in the chicken, and season to taste with salt. Simmer gently for 6–8 minutes, or until the chicken is heated through and the beans are tender. Transfer to warmed serving bowls, garnish with coriander sprigs and serve with freshly cooked rice.

Chicken Pepperonata

INGREDIENTS

8 skinless chicken thighs

2 tbsp wholemeal flour

2 tbsp olive oil

1 small onion, thinly sliced

1 garlic clove, crushed

1 each large red, yellow and green peppers, deseeded and thinly sliced

400 g/14 oz canned chopped tomatoes

1 tbsp chopped oregano, plus extra to garnish

salt and pepper

crusty wholemeal bread, to serve

serves ❹

1 Toss the chicken thighs in the flour, shaking off the excess.

2 Heat the oil in a wide frying pan and fry the chicken quickly until sealed and lightly browned, then remove from the pan.

3 Add the onion to the pan and gently fry until soft. Add the garlic, peppers, tomatoes and oregano, then bring to the boil, stirring.

4 Arrange the chicken over the vegetables, season well with salt and pepper, then cover the pan tightly and simmer for 20–25 minutes or until the chicken is completely cooked and tender.

5 Taste and adjust the seasoning if necessary, garnish with oregano and serve with crusty wholemeal bread.

Chicken Risotto with Saffron

INGREDIENTS

serves ❹

125 g/4½ oz butter

900 g/2 lb skinless, boneless chicken breasts, thinly sliced

1 large onion, chopped

500 g/1 lb 2 oz risotto rice

150 ml/5 fl oz white wine

1 tsp crumbled saffron threads

1.3 litres/2¼ pints chicken stock

55 g/2 oz freshly grated Parmesan cheese

salt and pepper

1 Heat 55 g/2 oz of the butter in a deep saucepan. Add the chicken and onion and cook, stirring frequently, for 8 minutes, or until golden brown.

2 Add the rice and mix to coat in the butter. Cook, stirring constantly for 2–3 minutes, or until the grains are translucent. Add the wine and cook, stirring constantly, for 1 minute until reduced.

3 Mix the saffron with 4 tablespoons of the hot stock. Add the liquid to the rice and cook, stirring constantly, until it is absorbed.

4 Gradually add the remaining hot stock, a ladle at a time. Stir constantly and add more liquid as the rice absorbs each addition. Cook for 20 minutes, or until all the liquid is absorbed and the rice is creamy. Season to taste.

5 Remove the risotto from the heat and add the remaining butter. Mix well, then stir in the Parmesan until it melts. Spoon the risotto onto warmed plates and serve immediately.

Mexican Turkey

INGREDIENTS

serves 4

55 g/2 oz plain flour

4 turkey breast fillets

3 tbsp corn oil

1 onion, thinly sliced

1 red pepper, deseeded and sliced

300 ml/10 fl oz chicken stock

25 g/1 oz raisins

4 tomatoes, peeled, deseeded and chopped

1 tsp chilli powder

½ tsp ground cinnamon

pinch of ground cumin

25 g/1 oz plain chocolate, finely chopped or grated

salt and pepper

sprigs of fresh coriander, to garnish

1 Preheat the oven to 160°C/325°F/Gas Mark 3. Spread the flour on a plate and season with salt and pepper. Coat the turkey fillets in the seasoned flour, shaking off any excess. Reserve the seasoned flour.

2 Heat the oil in a flameproof casserole. Add the turkey fillets and cook over a medium heat, turning occasionally, for 5–10 minutes, or until golden. Transfer to a plate with a slotted spoon.

3 Add the onion and red pepper to the casserole. Cook over a low heat, stirring occasionally, for 5 minutes, or until softened. Sprinkle in any remaining seasoned flour and cook, stirring constantly, for 1 minute. Gradually stir in the stock, then add the raisins, chopped tomatoes, chilli powder, cinnamon, cumin and chocolate. Season to taste with salt and pepper. Bring to the boil, stirring constantly.

4 Return the turkey to the casserole, cover and cook in the preheated oven for 50 minutes. Serve immediately, garnished with sprigs of coriander.

Italian Turkey Steaks

INGREDIENTS

serves 4

1 tbsp olive oil

4 turkey escalopes or steaks

2 red peppers, deseeded and sliced

1 red onion, sliced

2 garlic cloves, finely chopped

300 ml/10 fl oz passata

150 ml/5 fl oz medium white wine

1 tbsp chopped fresh marjoram

400 g/14 oz canned cannellini beans, drained and rinsed

3 tbsp fresh white breadcrumbs

salt and pepper

fresh basil sprigs, to garnish

1 Preheat the grill to medium. Heat the oil in a flameproof casserole or heavy-based frying pan. Add the turkey escalopes and cook over a medium heat for 5–10 minutes, turning occasionally, until golden. Transfer to a plate.

2 Add the red pepper and onion to the casserole and cook over a low heat, stirring occasionally, for 5 minutes, or until soft. Add the garlic and cook for a further 2 minutes.

3 Return the turkey to the casserole and add the passata, wine and marjoram. Season to taste with salt and pepper. Bring to the boil, then reduce the heat, cover and simmer, stirring occasionally, for 25–30 minutes, or until the turkey is cooked through and tender.

4 Stir in the cannellini beans and simmer for a further 5 minutes. Sprinkle the breadcrumbs over the top and place under the preheated grill for 2–3 minutes, or until golden. Serve, garnished with fresh basil sprigs.

Turkey in a Piquant Sauce

INGREDIENTS

serves ❹

2 tbsp plain flour

1 kg/2 lb 4 oz turkey pieces

25 g/1 oz butter

1 tbsp sunflower oil

2 onions, sliced

1 garlic clove, finely chopped

1 red pepper, deseeded and sliced

400 g/14 oz canned chopped tomatoes

1 bouquet garni

150 ml/5 fl oz chicken stock

salt and pepper

2 tbsp chopped fresh parsley, to garnish

1 Spread the flour on a plate and season with salt and pepper. Coat the turkey pieces in the seasoned flour, shaking off any excess.

2 Melt the butter with the oil in a flameproof casserole or large saucepan. Add the turkey and cook over a medium heat, stirring, for 5–10 minutes, or until golden. Transfer the turkey pieces to a plate with a slotted spoon and keep warm. Add the onions, garlic and red pepper to the casserole and cook, stirring occasionally, for 5 minutes, or until softened. Sprinkle in any remaining flour and cook, stirring constantly, for 1 minute.

3 Return the turkey pieces to the casserole, then add the tomatoes and their juices, the bouquet garni and stock. Bring to the boil, stirring constantly, then cover and simmer for 1¼ hours, or until the turkey is cooked through and tender.

4 Transfer the turkey to a serving platter with a slotted spoon. Remove and discard the bouquet garni. Return the sauce to the boil and cook until reduced and thickened. Season to taste with salt and pepper and pour over the turkey. Serve immediately, garnished with parsley.

Stir-Fried Turkey with Cranberry Glaze

INGREDIENTS

serves ④

450g/1lb boneless turkey breast

2 tbsp sunflower oil

15 g/½ oz stem ginger

50 g/1¾ oz fresh or frozen cranberries

100 g/3½ oz canned chestnuts

4 tbsp cranberry sauce

3 tbsp light soy sauce

salt and pepper

1 Remove any skin from the turkey breast. Using a sharp knife, thinly slice the turkey breast.

2 Heat the sunflower oil in a large preheated wok or heavy-based frying pan.

3 Add the turkey to the wok and stir-fry for 5 minutes, or until cooked through.

4 Drain off the syrup from the stem ginger. Using a sharp knife, chop the ginger finely.

5 Add the ginger and the cranberries to the wok and stir-fry for 2–3 minutes, or until the cranberries have softened.

6 Add the chestnuts, cranberry sauce and soy sauce, season to taste with salt and pepper and allow to bubble for 2–3 minutes.

7 Transfer the glazed turkey stir-fry to individual warmed serving dishes and serve immediately.

Orange Turkey with Rice

INGREDIENTS

serves **4**

1 tbsp olive oil

1 onion, chopped

450 g/1 lb skinless lean turkey (such as fillet), cut into thin strips

300 ml/10 fl oz unsweetened orange juice

1 bay leaf

225 g/8 oz small broccoli florets

1 large courgette, diced

1 large orange

350 g/12 oz cooked brown rice

salt and pepper

25 g/1 oz stoned black olives in brine, drained and quartered, and shredded basil leaves, to garnish

tomato and onion salad, to serve

1 Heat the oil in a large frying pan and fry the onion and turkey, stirring, for 4–5 minutes until lightly browned.

2 Pour in the orange juice and add the bay leaf and seasoning. Bring to the boil and simmer for 10 minutes.

3 Meanwhile, bring a large saucepan of water to the boil, add the broccoli florets and cook, covered, for 2 minutes. Add the diced courgette, bring back to the boil, cover and cook for 3 minutes (do not overcook). Drain and set aside.

4 Using a sharp knife, peel off the skin and white pith from the orange.

5 Thinly slice down the orange to make round slices, then halve each slice.

6 Stir the broccoli, courgette, rice and orange slices into the turkey mixture. Gently mix together and season, then heat through for a further 3–4 minutes until piping hot.

7 Transfer the turkey rice to warmed serving plates and garnish with black olives and shredded basil leaves. Serve with a tomato and onion salad.

Duck Legs with Olives

INGREDIENTS

serves **4**

4 duck legs, all visible fat trimmed off

800 g/1 lb 12 oz canned tomatoes, chopped

8 garlic cloves, peeled, but left whole

1 large onion, chopped

1 carrot, finely chopped

1 celery stick, finely chopped

3 sprigs fresh thyme

100 g/3½ oz Spanish green olives in brine, stuffed with pimientos, garlic or almonds, drained and rinsed

1 tsp finely grated orange rind

salt and pepper

1 Put the duck legs in the bottom of a flameproof casserole or a large, heavy-based frying pan with a tight-fitting lid. Add the tomatoes, garlic, onion, carrot, celery, thyme and olives and stir together. Season to taste with salt and pepper.

2 Turn the heat to high and cook, uncovered, until the ingredients begin to bubble. Reduce the heat to low, cover tightly and simmer for 1¼–1½ hours until the duck is very tender. Check occasionally and add a little water if the mixture appears to be drying out.

3 Preheat the oven to 160°C/325°F/Gas Mark 3. When the duck is tender, transfer it to a serving platter, cover and keep hot in the preheated oven. Leave the casserole uncovered, increase the heat to medium and cook, stirring, for about 10 minutes until the mixture forms a sauce. Stir in the orange rind, then taste and adjust the seasoning if necessary.

4 Mash the tender garlic cloves with a fork and spread over the duck legs. Spoon the sauce over the top. Serve at once.

Braised Asian Duck

INGREDIENTS

serves **4**

3 tbsp soy sauce

¼ tsp **Chinese five-spice powder**

4 duck legs or breasts, cut into pieces

3 tbsp vegetable oil

1 tsp dark sesame oil

1 tsp finely chopped fresh ginger

1 large garlic clove, finely chopped

4 spring onions, white parts sliced thickly, green part shredded

2 tbsp rice wine or dry sherry

1 tbsp oyster sauce

3 whole star anise

2 tsp black peppercorns

450–600 ml/16 fl oz–1 pint chicken stock or water

2 tbsp cornflour

salt and pepper

1 Combine 1 tablespoon of the soy sauce, the five-spice powder, and salt and pepper to taste and rub over the duck pieces. Brown the duck pieces in a casserole with 2½ tablespoons of the vegetable oil, remove and transfer to a plate.

2 Drain the fat from the casserole and wipe out. Heat the sesame oil and remaining vegetable oil. Add the ginger and garlic. Cook for a few seconds. Add the white spring onion. Cook for a few seconds. Return the duck to the casserole. Add the rice wine, oyster sauce, star anise, peppercorns and remaining soy sauce. Pour in enough stock to just cover. Bring to the boil, cover and simmer gently for 1½ hours, adding more water if necessary.

3 Mix the cornflour with 2 tablespoons of the cooking liquid to a smooth paste. Add to the remaining liquid, stirring until thickened. Garnish with the green spring onion shreds to serve.

3 Fish & Seafood

Fish and seafood make mouthwatering one-pot soups and stews. Try firm-fleshed chunks of white fish and plump juicy mussels and prawns in French bouillabaise or a Moroccan fish tagine. Equally delicious are seafood and rice, easily cooked from start to finish in a wide deep pan. For maximum flavour try baking firm-fleshed fish in the simplest container of all, a sealed paper or foil package that retains every bit of flavour.

Bouillabaisse

INGREDIENTS

serves **4**

200 g/7 oz live mussels

100 ml/3½ fl oz olive oil

3 garlic cloves, chopped

2 onions, chopped

2 tomatoes, deseeded and chopped

700 ml/1¼ pints fish stock

400 ml/14 fl oz white wine

1 bay leaf

pinch of saffron threads

2 tbsp chopped fresh basil

2 tbsp chopped fresh parsley

250 g/9 oz snapper or monkfish fillets

250 g/9 oz haddock fillets, skinned

200 g/7 oz prawns, peeled and deveined

100 g/3½ oz scallops

salt and pepper

fresh baguettes, to serve

1 Soak the mussels in lightly salted water for 10 minutes. Scrub the shells under cold running water and pull off any beards. Discard any with broken shells. Tap the remaining mussels and discard any that refuse to close. Put the rest into a large saucepan with a little water, bring to the boil and cook over high heat for 4 minutes. Transfer the cooked mussels to a bowl, discarding any that remain closed, and reserve. Wipe out the pan with kitchen paper.

2 Heat the oil in the pan over a medium heat. Add the garlic and onions and cook, stirring, for 3 minutes. Stir in the tomatoes, stock, wine, bay leaf, saffron and herbs. Bring to the boil, reduce the heat, cover and simmer for 30 minutes.

3 When the tomato mixture is cooked, rinse the fish fillets, pat dry and cut into chunks. Add to the pan and simmer for 5 minutes. Add the mussels, prawns and scallops and season with salt and pepper. Cook for 3 minutes, until the fish is cooked through.

4 Remove from the heat, discard the bay leaf and ladle into serving bowls. Serve with fresh baguettes.

Mediterranean Fish Stew

INGREDIENTS

serves 4

2 tbsp olive oil

1 onion, sliced

pinch of saffron threads, lightly crushed

1 tbsp chopped fresh thyme

2 garlic cloves, finely chopped

800 g/1 lb 12 oz canned chopped tomatoes, drained

2 litres/3½ pints fish stock

175 ml/6 fl oz dry white wine

350 g/12 oz red mullet fillets, cut into chunks

450 g/1 lb monkfish fillets, cut into chunks

450 g/1 lb fresh clams, scrubbed

225 g/8 oz squid rings

2 tbsp fresh basil leaves, plus extra to garnish

salt and pepper

1 Heat the oil in a large, flameproof casserole. Add the onion, saffron, thyme and a pinch of salt. Cook over a low heat, stirring occasionally, for 5 minutes, or until the onion has softened.

2 Add the garlic and cook for a further 2 minutes, then add the drained tomatoes and pour in the stock and wine. Season to taste with salt and pepper, bring the mixture to the boil, then reduce the heat and simmer for 15 minutes.

3 Add the chunks of mullet and monkfish and simmer for 3 minutes. Add the clams and squid and simmer for 5 minutes, or until the clam shells have opened. Discard any clams that remain closed. Tear in the basil and stir. Serve garnished with the extra basil leaves.

Seafood in Saffron Sauce

INGREDIENTS

serves **4**

225 g/8 oz live mussels

225 g/8 oz live clams

2 tbsp olive oil

1 onion, sliced

pinch of saffron threads

1 tbsp chopped fresh thyme

2 garlic cloves, finely chopped

800 g/1 lb 12 oz canned tomatoes, drained and chopped

175 ml/6 fl oz dry white wine

2 litres/3½ pints fish stock

350 g/12 oz red mullet fillets, cut into bite-sized chunks

450 g/1 lb monkfish fillets, cut into bite-sized chunks

225 g/8 oz raw squid rings

2 tbsp shredded fresh basil leaves

salt and pepper

fresh bread, to serve

1 Clean the mussels and clams by scrubbing or scraping the shells and pulling out any beards that are attached to the mussels. Discard any with broken shells or any that refuse to close when tapped.

2 Heat the oil in a large, flameproof casserole and cook the onion with the saffron, thyme and a pinch of salt over a low heat, stirring occasionally, for 5 minutes, or until soft. Add the garlic and cook, stirring, for 2 minutes.

3 Add the tomatoes, wine and stock, season to taste with salt and pepper and stir well. Bring to the boil, then reduce the heat and simmer for 15 minutes.

4 Add the fish chunks and simmer for a further 3 minutes. Add the clams, mussels and squid rings and simmer for a further 5 minutes, or until the mussels and clams have opened. Discard any that remain closed. Stir in the basil and serve immediately, accompanied by plenty of fresh bread to mop up the broth.

Moroccan Fish Tagine

INGREDIENTS

serves ❹

2 tbsp olive oil

1 large onion, finely chopped

pinch of saffron threads

½ tsp ground cinnamon

1 tsp ground coriander

½ tsp ground cumin

½ tsp ground turmeric

200 g/7 oz canned chopped tomatoes

300 ml/10 fl oz fish stock

4 small red mullet, cleaned, boned and heads and tails removed

55 g/2 oz stoned green olives

1 tbsp chopped preserved lemon

3 tbsp chopped fresh coriander

salt and pepper

freshly cooked couscous, to serve

1 Heat the olive oil in a flameproof casserole. Add the onion and cook gently over a very low heat, stirring occasionally, for 10 minutes, or until soft, but not coloured. Add the saffron, cinnamon, ground coriander, cumin and turmeric and cook for a further 30 seconds, stirring constantly.

2 Add the tomatoes and fish stock and stir well. Bring to the boil, reduce the heat, cover and simmer for 15 minutes. Uncover and simmer for 20–35 minutes, or until thickened.

3 Cut each red mullet in half, then add the fish pieces to the casserole, pushing them down into the liquid. Simmer the stew for a further 5–6 minutes, or until the fish is just cooked.

4 Carefully stir in the olives, preserved lemon and chopped coriander. Season to taste with salt and pepper and serve immediately with some couscous.

Moules Marinières

INGREDIENTS

serves **4**

2 kg/4 lb 8 oz live mussels

300 ml/10 fl oz dry white wine

6 shallots, finely chopped

1 bouquet garni

pepper

4 bay leaves, to garnish

crusty bread, to serve

1 Clean the mussels by scrubbing or scraping the shells and pulling off any beards. Discard any with broken shells or any that refuse to close when tapped with a knife. Rinse the mussels under cold running water.

2 Pour the wine into a large, heavy-based saucepan, add the shallots and bouquet garni and season to taste with pepper. Bring to the boil over a medium heat. Add the mussels, cover tightly and cook, shaking the pan occasionally, for 5 minutes. Remove and discard the bouquet garni and any mussels that remain closed.

3 Strain the cooking liquid through a muslin-lined sieve, then transfer to a clean saucepan and reheat. Divide the mussels between 4 soup plates with a slotted spoon. Spoon the hot cooking liquid over the mussels, garnish with a bay leaf, and serve immediately with bread.

Squid with Parsley & Pine Kernels

INGREDIENTS

serves 4

85 g/3 oz sultanas

5 tbsp olive oil

6 tbsp chopped fresh
flat-leaf parsley, plus extra
to garnish

2 garlic cloves, finely
chopped

800 g/1 lb 12 oz prepared
squid, sliced, or squid rings

125 ml/4 fl oz dry white wine

500 g/1 lb 2 oz passata

pinch of chilli powder

pinch of salt

85 g/3 oz pine kernels,
finely chopped

1 Place the sultanas in a small bowl, cover with lukewarm water and set aside for 15 minutes to plump up.

2 Meanwhile, heat the olive oil in a heavy-based saucepan. Add the parsley and garlic and cook over a low heat, stirring frequently, for 3 minutes. Add the squid and cook, stirring occasionally, for 5 minutes.

3 Increase the heat to medium, pour in the wine and cook until it has almost completely evaporated. Stir in the passata and season to taste with chilli powder and salt. Reduce the heat, cover and simmer gently, stirring occasionally, for 45–50 minutes, until the squid is almost tender.

4 Drain the sultanas and stir them into the pan with the pine kernels. Leave to simmer for a further 10 minutes, then serve immediately, garnished with the reserved chopped parsley.

Jambalaya

INGREDIENTS

serves 4

2 tbsp vegetable oil

1 green pepper, deseeded
and roughly chopped

2 celery sticks, roughly
chopped

3 garlic cloves, chopped
finely

2 tsp paprika

300 g/1½ oz skinless,
boneless chicken breasts,
chopped

100 g/3½ oz kabanos
sausages, chopped

3 tomatoes, peeled and
chopped

450 g/1 lb long-grain rice

850 ml/1½ pints hot chicken
or fish stock

1 tsp dried oregano

2 bay leaves

12 large raw prawns

2 tbsp chopped fresh
parsley

salt and pepper

1 Heat the vegetable oil in a large frying pan over a low heat. Add the pepper, celery and garlic and cook for 8–10 minutes until all the vegetables have softened. Add the paprika and cook for a further 30 seconds. Add the chicken and sausages and cook for 8–10 minutes until lightly browned. Add the tomatoes and cook for 2–3 minutes until they have collapsed.

2 Add the rice to the pan and stir well. Pour in the hot stock, oregano and bay leaves and stir well. Cover and simmer for 10 minutes.

3 Add the prawns and stir. Cover again and cook for a further 6–8 minutes until the rice is tender and the prawns are cooked through.

4 Stir in the parsley and season to taste with salt and pepper. Transfer to a large serving dish and serve.

Prawns with Coconut Rice

INGREDIENTS

serves **4**

115 g/4 oz dried **Chinese mushrooms**

2 tbsp vegetable or groundnut oil

6 spring onions, chopped

55 g/2 oz desiccated coconut

1 fresh green chilli, deseeded and chopped

225 g/8 oz jasmine rice

150 ml/5 fl oz fish stock

400 ml/14 fl oz coconut milk

350 g/12 oz cooked peeled prawns

6 sprigs fresh Thai basil

1 Place the mushrooms in a small bowl, cover with hot water and set aside to soak for 30 minutes. Drain, then cut off and discard the stalks and slice the caps.

2 Heat the oil in a wok and stir-fry the spring onions, coconut and chilli for 2–3 minutes, until lightly browned. Add the mushrooms and stir-fry for 3–4 minutes.

3 Add the rice and stir-fry for 2–3 minutes, then add the stock and bring to the boil. Reduce the heat and add the coconut milk. Simmer for 10–15 minutes, until the rice is tender. Stir in the prawns and basil, heat through and serve.

Seafood Risotto

INGREDIENTS

1 tbsp olive oil

55 g/2 oz butter

2 garlic cloves, chopped

350 g/12 oz risotto rice

1.3 litres/2¼ pints fish or chicken stock

250 g/9 oz mixed cooked seafood, such as prawns, squid, mussels and clams

2 tbsp chopped fresh oregano, plus extra to garnish

55 g/2 oz freshly grated pecorino or Parmesan cheese

salt and pepper

serves ❹

1 Heat the oil with half of the butter in a deep saucepan over a medium heat until the butter has melted. Add the garlic and cook, stirring, for 1 minute.

2 Reduce the heat, add the rice and mix to coat in oil and butter. Cook, stirring constantly, for 2–3 minutes, or until the grains are translucent.

3 Gradually add the hot stock, a ladle at a time. Stir constantly and add more liquid as the rice absorbs each addition. Increase the heat to medium so that the liquid bubbles. Cook for 20 minutes, or until all the liquid is absorbed and the rice is creamy.

4 About 5 minutes before the rice is ready, add the seafood and oregano to the pan and mix well.

5 Remove the pan from the heat and season to taste. Add the remaining butter and mix well, then stir in the grated cheese until it melts. Spoon onto warmed plates and serve immediately, garnished with extra oregano.

Fish & Rice with Dark Rum

INGREDIENTS

serves ❹

450 g/1 lb firm white fish fillets (such as cod or monkfish), skinned and cut into 2.5-cm/1-inch cubes

2 tsp ground cumin

2 tsp dried oregano

2 tbsp lime juice

150 ml/5 fl oz dark rum

1 tbsp dark muscovado sugar

3 garlic cloves, finely chopped

1 large onion, chopped

1 each medium red pepper, green pepper, yellow pepper, deseeded and sliced into rings

1.2 litres/2 pints fish stock

350 g/12 oz long-grain rice

salt and pepper

fresh oregano leaves, and lime wedges to garnish

crusty bread, to serve

1 Place the cubes of fish in a bowl and add the cumin, oregano, lime juice, rum and sugar. Season to taste with salt and pepper. Mix thoroughly, cover with clingfilm and set aside to chill for 2 hours.

2 Meanwhile, place the garlic, onion and peppers in a large saucepan. Pour in the stock and stir in the rice. Bring to the boil, reduce the heat cover and simmer for 15 minutes.

3 Gently stir in the fish and the marinade juices. Bring back to the boil and simmer, uncovered, stirring occasionally but taking care not to break up the fish, for about 10 minutes until the fish is cooked through and the rice is tender.

4 Season to taste with salt and pepper and transfer to a warmed serving plate. Garnish with fresh oregano and lime wedges and serve with crusty bread.

Sicilian Tuna

INGREDIENTS

serves 4

**4 tuna steaks, about
140 g/5 oz each**

**2 fennel bulbs, thickly sliced
lengthways**

2 red onions, sliced

2 tbsp extra virgin olive oil

crusty rolls, to serve

MARINADE

**125 ml/4 fl oz extra virgin
olive oil**

**4 garlic cloves, finely
chopped**

**4 fresh red chillies, deseeded
and finely chopped**

**juice and finely grated rind
of 2 lemons**

**4 tbsp finely chopped fresh
flat-leaf parsley**

salt and pepper

1 Whisk all the marinade ingredients together in a small bowl. Put the tuna steaks in a large, shallow dish and spoon over 4 tablespoons of the marinade, turning until well coated. Cover and leave to marinate in the refrigerator for 30 minutes. Reserve the remaining marinade.

2 Heat a ridged griddle pan over a high heat. Put the fennel and onions in a separate bowl, add the oil and toss well to coat. Add to the griddle pan and cook for 5 minutes on each side until just beginning to colour. Transfer to 4 warmed serving plates, drizzle with the reserved marinade and keep warm.

3 Add the tuna steaks to the griddle pan and cook, turning once, for 4–5 minutes until firm to the touch but still moist inside. Transfer the tuna to the serving plates and serve immediately with crusty rolls.

Swordfish with Tomatoes & Olives

INGREDIENTS

2 tbsp olive oil

1 onion, finely chopped

1 celery stick, finely chopped

115 g/4 oz green olives, stoned

450 g/1 lb tomatoes, chopped

3 tbsp bottled capers, drained

4 swordfish steaks, about 140 g/5 oz each

salt and pepper

fresh flat-leaf parsley sprigs, to garnish

serves ❹

1 Heat the oil in a large, heavy-based frying pan. Add the onion and celery and cook over a low heat, stirring occasionally, for 5 minutes, or until soft.

2 Meanwhile, roughly chop half the olives. Stir the chopped and whole olives into the pan with the tomatoes and capers and season to taste with salt and pepper.

3 Bring to the boil, then reduce the heat, cover and simmer gently, stirring occasionally, for 15 minutes.

4 Add the swordfish steaks to the pan and return to the boil. Cover and simmer, turning the fish once, for 20 minutes, or until the fish is cooked and the flesh flakes easily. Transfer the fish to serving plates and spoon the sauce over them. Garnish with fresh parsley sprigs and serve immediately.

Monkfish Parcels

INGREDIENTS

serves **4**

4 tsp olive oil

2 courgettes, sliced

1 large red pepper, peeled, deseeded and cut into strips

2 monkfish fillets, about 125 g/4½ oz each, skin and membrane removed

6 smoked streaky bacon rashers

salt and pepper

freshly cooked pasta and slices of olive bread, to serve

1 Preheat the oven to 190°C/375°F/Gas Mark 5. Cut 4 large pieces of foil, each about 23 cm/ 9 inches square. Brush them lightly with a little of the oil, then divide the courgettes and pepper between them.

2 Rinse the fish fillets under cold running water and pat dry with kitchen paper. Cut them in half, then put 1 piece on top of each pile of courgettes and pepper. Cut the bacon rashers in half and lay 3 pieces across each piece of fish. Season to taste with salt and pepper, drizzle over the remaining oil and close up the parcels. Seal tightly, transfer to an ovenproof dish and bake in the preheated oven for 25 minutes.

3 Remove from the oven, open each foil parcel slightly and serve with pasta and slices of olive bread.

Roasted Monkfish

INGREDIENTS

serves 4

675 g/1 lb 8 oz monkfish tail, skinned

4–5 large garlic cloves, peeled

3 tbsp olive oil

1 onion, cut into wedges

1 aubergine, about 300 g/10½ oz, cut into chunks

1 red pepper, deseeded, cut into wedges

1 yellow pepper, deseeded, cut into wedges

1 large courgette, about 225 g/8 oz, cut into wedges

salt and pepper

1 tbsp shredded fresh basil, to garnish

1 Preheat the oven to 200°C/400°F/Gas Mark 6. Remove the central bone from the fish if not already removed and make small slits down each fillet. Cut 2 of the garlic cloves into thin slivers and insert into the fish. Place the fish on a sheet of greaseproof paper, season with salt and pepper to taste and drizzle over 1 tablespoon of the oil. Bring the top edges together. Form into a pleat and fold over, then fold the ends underneath, completely encasing the fish. Reserve.

2 Put the remaining garlic cloves and all the vegetables into a roasting tin and drizzle with the remaining oil, turning the vegetables so that they are well coated in the oil.

3 Roast in the preheated oven for 20 minutes, turning occasionally. Put the fish parcel on top of the vegetables and cook for a further 15–20 minutes, or until the vegetables are tender and the fish is cooked.

4 Remove from the oven and open up the parcel. Cut the monkfish into thick slices. Arrange the vegetables on warmed serving plates, top with the fish slices and sprinkle with the basil. Serve immediately.

Roasted Seafood

INGREDIENTS

serves 4

600 g/1 lb 5 oz new potatoes

3 red onions, cut into wedges

2 courgettes, cut into chunks

8 garlic cloves, peeled but left whole

2 lemons, cut into wedges

4 fresh rosemary sprigs

4 tbsp olive oil

350 g/12 oz unpeeled raw prawns

2 small raw squid, cut into rings

4 tomatoes, quartered

1 Preheat the oven to 200°C/400°F/Gas Mark 6.

2 Scrub the potatoes to remove any dirt. Cut any large potatoes in half. Bring a large saucepan of lightly salted water to the boil, add the potatoes and cook for 10-15 minutes. Place the potatoes in a large roasting tin together with the onions, courgettes, garlic, lemons and rosemary sprigs.

3 Pour over the oil and toss to coat all the vegetables in it. Roast in the oven for 30 minutes, turning occasionally, until the potatoes are tender.

4 Once the potatoes are tender, add the prawns, squid and tomatoes, tossing to coat them in the oil, and roast for 5 minutes. All the vegetables should be cooked through and slightly charred for full flavour. Transfer the roasted seafood and vegetables to warmed serving plates and serve hot.

Spicy Scallops with Lime & Chilli

INGREDIENTS

serves **4**

16 large scallops

1 tbsp butter

1 tbsp vegetable oil

1 tsp crushed garlic

1 tsp grated fresh ginger

1 bunch of spring onions, thinly sliced

finely grated rind of 1 lime

1 small fresh red chilli, deseeded and very finely chopped

3 tbsp lime juice

lime wedges and freshly cooked rice, to serve

1 Trim the scallops, then wash and pat dry. Separate the corals from the white parts, then slice each white part in half horizontally, making 2 rounds.

2 Heat the butter and oil in a wok or frying pan. Add the garlic and ginger and stir-fry for 1 minute without browning. Add the spring onions and stir-fry for 1 further minute.

3 Add the scallops and stir-fry over a high heat for 4–5 minutes. Stir in the lime rind, chilli and lime juice and cook for 1 further minute.

4 Serve the scallops hot, with the juices spooned over them, accompanied by lime wedges and cooked rice.

Fresh Baked Sardines

INGREDIENTS

2 tbsp olive oil

2 large onions, sliced into rings

3 garlic cloves, chopped

2 large courgettes, cut into sticks

3 tbsp fresh thyme, stalks removed

8 large sardine fillets

115 g/4 oz grated Parmesan cheese

4 eggs, beaten

300 ml/10 fl oz milk

salt and pepper

serves 4

1 Heat 1 tablespoon of the olive oil in a frying pan. Add the onion rings and chopped garlic and fry over a low heat, stirring occasionally, for 2–3 minutes, until soft and translucent.

2 Add the courgettes to the pan and cook, stirring occasionally, for about 5 minutes, or until turning golden. Stir 2 tablespoons of the thyme leaves into the mixture and remove from the heat.

3 Place half the onions and courgettes in the base of a large ovenproof dish. Top with the sardine fillets and half the grated Parmesan cheese. Place the remaining onions and courgettes on top and sprinkle with the remaining thyme.

4 Mix the eggs and milk together in a bowl and season to taste with salt and pepper. Pour the mixture into the dish. Sprinkle the remaining Parmesan cheese over the top.

5 Bake in a preheated oven, 180°C/350°F/Gas Mark 4 for 20–25 minutes, or until golden and set. Serve the fresh baked sardines hot.

4 Vegetables

Thick hearty vegetable soups such as
minestrone or French onion soup provide a
satisfying meal-in-a-bowl, while the earthy
mellow flavours of beans and grains
combine with fresh vegetables to make
nutritious and deeply satisfying stews.
There are also recipes in this chapter for
risottos and gratins, Asian-style egg-fried
rice and an irresistible vegetable pie. All can
be prepared in only one pot, dish or pan,
leaving you with a minimum of washing up.

Chunky Vegetable Soup

INGREDIENTS

serves 6

2 carrots, sliced

1 onion, diced

1 garlic clove, crushed

350 g/12 oz new potatoes, diced

2 celery sticks, sliced

115 g/4 oz closed-cup mushrooms, quartered

400 g/14 oz canned chopped tomatoes in tomato juice

600 ml/1 pint vegetable stock

1 bay leaf

1 tsp dried mixed herbs or 1 tbsp chopped fresh mixed herbs

85 g/3 oz sweetcorn kernels, frozen or canned, drained

55 g/2 oz green cabbage, shredded

pepper

crusty wholemeal or white bread rolls, to serve

1 Put the carrots, onion, garlic, potatoes, celery, mushrooms, tomatoes and stock into a large saucepan. Stir in the bay leaf and herbs. Bring to the boil, then reduce the heat, cover and simmer for 25 minutes.

2 Add the sweetcorn and cabbage and return to the boil. Reduce the heat, cover and simmer for 5 minutes, or until the vegetables are tender. Remove and discard the bay leaf. Season to taste with pepper.

3 Ladle into warmed bowls and serve at once with crusty bread rolls.

Minestrone

INGREDIENTS

serves ❹

2 tbsp olive oil

2 garlic cloves, chopped

2 red onions, chopped

75 g/2¾ oz **Parma ham**, sliced

1 red pepper, deseeded and chopped

1 orange pepper, deseeded and chopped

400 g/14 oz canned chopped tomatoes

1 litre/1¾ pints vegetable stock

1 celery stick, trimmed and sliced

400 g/14 oz canned borlotti beans

100 g/3½ oz green leafy cabbage, shredded

75 g/2¾ oz frozen peas, thawed

1 tbsp chopped fresh parsley

75 g/2¾ oz dried vermicelli

salt and pepper

freshly grated **Parmesan** cheese, to garnish

fresh crusty bread, to serve

1 Heat the oil in a large saucepan. Add the garlic, onions and Parma ham and cook over a medium heat, stirring, for 3 minutes, until slightly softened. Add the red and orange peppers and the chopped tomatoes and cook for a further 2 minutes, stirring. Stir in the stock, then add the celery. Drain and add the borlotti beans along with the cabbage, peas and parsley. Season with salt and pepper. Bring to the boil, then reduce the heat and simmer for 30 minutes.

2 Add the vermicelli to the pan. Cook for a further 10–12 minutes, or according to the packet instructions. Remove from the heat and ladle into serving bowls. Garnish with freshly grated Parmesan cheese and serve with fresh crusty bread.

French Onion Soup

INGREDIENTS

serves 6

675 g/1 lb 8 oz onions

3 tbsp olive oil

4 garlic cloves, 3 chopped and 1 peeled but kept whole

1 tsp sugar

2 tsp chopped fresh thyme

2 tbsp plain flour

125 ml/4 fl oz dry white wine

2 litres/3½ pints vegetable stock

6 slices of French bread

300 g/10½ oz Gruyère cheese, grated

fresh thyme sprigs, to garnish

1 Thinly slice the onions. Heat the olive oil in a large, heavy-based saucepan, then add the onions and cook, stirring occasionally, for 10 minutes, until they are just beginning to brown. Stir in the chopped garlic, sugar and thyme, then reduce the heat and cook, stirring occasionally, for 30 minutes, or until the onions are golden brown.

2 Sprinkle in the flour and cook, stirring, for 1–2 minutes. Stir in the wine. Gradually stir in the stock and bring to the boil, skimming off any scum that rises to the surface, then reduce the heat and simmer for 45 minutes. Meanwhile, preheat the grill to medium. Toast the bread on both sides under the grill. Rub the toast with the garlic clove.

3 Ladle the soup into 6 flameproof bowls set on a baking sheet. Float a piece of toast in each bowl and divide the grated cheese between them. Place under the preheated grill for 2–3 minutes, or until the cheese has just melted. Garnish with thyme and serve.

Borscht

INGREDIENTS

serves 6

1 onion

55 g/2 oz butter

350 g/12 oz raw beetroot, cut into thin batons, and 1 raw beetroot, grated

1 carrot, cut into thin batons

3 celery sticks, thinly sliced

2 tomatoes, peeled, deseeded and chopped

1.4 litres/2½ pints vegetable stock

1 tbsp white wine vinegar

1 tbsp sugar

2 tbsp snipped fresh dill

115 g/4 oz white cabbage, shredded

salt and pepper

150 ml/5 fl oz soured cream, to garnish

crusty bread, to serve

1 Slice the onion into rings. Melt the butter in a large, heavy-based saucepan. Add the onion and cook over a low heat, stirring occasionally, for 3–5 minutes, or until soft. Add the beetroot batons, carrot, celery and chopped tomatoes and cook, stirring frequently, for 4–5 minutes.

2 Add the stock, vinegar, sugar and 1 tablespoon of the snipped dill to the pan. Season to taste with salt and pepper. Bring to the boil, reduce the heat and simmer for 35–40 minutes, or until the vegetables are tender.

3 Stir in the cabbage, cover and simmer for 10 minutes. Stir in the grated beetroot, with any juices, and cook for a further 10 minutes. Ladle into warmed bowls. Garnish with a spoonful of soured cream and the other tablespoon of snipped dill and serve with crusty bread.

Vegetable Soup with Pesto

INGREDIENTS

1 litre/1¾ pints fresh cold water

bouquet garni of 1 fresh parsley sprig, 1 fresh thyme sprig, and 1 bay leaf, tied together with clean string

2 celery stalks, chopped

3 baby leeks, chopped

4 baby carrots, chopped

150 g/5½ oz new potatoes, scrubbed and cut into bite-sized chunks

4 tbsp shelled broad beans or peas

175 g/6 oz canned cannellini or flageolet beans, drained and rinsed

3 heads pak choi

150 g/5½ oz rocket

55 g/2 oz ready-made green pesto

pepper

serves ❹

1 Put the water and bouquet garni into a large saucepan and add the celery, leeks, carrots and potatoes. Bring to the boil, then reduce the heat and simmer for 10 minutes.

2 Stir in the broad beans or peas and canned beans and simmer for a further 10 minutes. Stir in the pak choi and rocket, season with pepper and simmer for a further 2–3 minutes. Remove and discard the bouquet garni.

3 Stir most of the pesto into the soup, then ladle into warmed bowls. Top with the remaining pesto and serve at once.

Spring Stew

INGREDIENTS

serves ❹

2 tbsp olive oil

4–8 baby onions, halved

2 celery sticks, sliced

225 g/8 oz baby carrots, scrubbed, and halved if large

300 g/10½ oz new potatoes, scrubbed and halved, or quartered if large

850 ml–1.2 litres/1½–2 pints vegetable stock

400 g/14 oz canned haricot beans, drained and rinsed

1½–2 tbsp light soy sauce

85 g/3 oz baby sweetcorn

115 g/4 oz fresh broad beans

½–1 Savoy cabbage

1½ tbsp cornflour

2 tbsp cold water

salt and pepper

55–85 g/2–3 oz Parmesan cheese or mature Cheddar cheese, grated, to serve

1 Heat the oil in a large, heavy-based saucepan, with a tight-fitting lid. Add the onions, celery, carrots and potatoes and cook, stirring frequently, for 5 minutes, or until soft. Add the stock, drained beans and soy sauce, then bring to the boil. Reduce the heat, cover and simmer for 12 minutes.

2 Add the baby sweetcorn and broad beans and season to taste with salt and pepper. Simmer for a further 3 minutes.

3 Meanwhile, discard the outer leaves and hard central core from the cabbage and shred the leaves. Add to the pan and simmer for a further 3–5 minutes, or until all the vegetables are tender.

4 Blend the cornflour with the water, stir into the pan and cook, stirring, for 4–6 minutes, or until the liquid has thickened. Serve with a bowl of cheese for stirring into the stew.

Tuscan Bean Stew

INGREDIENTS

serves 4

1 large fennel bulb

2 tbsp olive oil

1 red onion, cut into small wedges

2–4 garlic cloves, sliced

1 small aubergine, about 225 g/8 oz, cut into chunks

2 tbsp tomato purée

450–600 ml/16 fl oz–1 pint vegetable stock

450 g/1 lb ripe tomatoes

a few sprigs fresh oregano

400 g/14 oz canned borlotti beans

400 g/14 oz canned flageolet beans

1 yellow pepper, deseeded and cut into small strips

1 courgette, sliced into half moons

55 g/2 oz stoned black olives

25 g/1 oz Parmesan cheese, freshly shaved

salt and pepper

crusty bread, to serve

1 Trim the fennel and reserve any feathery fronds, then cut the bulb into small strips. Heat the oil in a large, heavy-based saucepan with a tight-fitting lid, and cook the onion, garlic and fennel strips, stirring frequently, for 5–8 minutes, or until softened.

2 Add the aubergine and cook, stirring frequently, for 5 minutes. Blend the tomato purée with a little of the stock in a jug and pour over the fennel mixture, then add the remaining stock, and the tomatoes and oregano. Bring to the boil, then reduce the heat, cover and simmer for 15 minutes, or until the tomatoes have begun to collapse.

3 Drain and rinse the beans, the drain again. Add them to the pan with the yellow pepper, courgette and olives. Simmer for a further 15 minutes, or until all the vegetables are tender. Taste and adjust the seasoning. Scatter with the Parmesan cheese shavings and serve garnished with the reserved fennel fronds, accompanied by crusty bread.

Chilli Bean Stew

INGREDIENTS

serves **4**–**6**

2 tbsp olive oil

1 onion, chopped

2–4 garlic cloves, chopped

2 fresh red chillies,
deseeded and sliced

225 g/8 oz canned kidney
beans, drained and rinsed

225 g/8 oz canned cannelini
beans, drained and rinsed

225 g/8 oz canned chickpeas,
drained and rinsed

1 tbsp tomato purée

850 ml/1½ pints stock

1 red pepper, deseeded and
chopped

4 tomatoes, roughly chopped

175 g/6 oz fresh broad beans

1 tbsp chopped fresh
coriander

pepper

soured cream, to serve

chopped coriander and
paprika, to garnish

1 Heat the oil in a large, heavy-based saucepan with a tight-fitting lid and cook the onion, garlic and chillies, stirring frequently, for 5 minutes, or until soft. Add the kidney and cannellini beans and the chickpeas. Blend the tomato purée with a little of the stock in a jug and pour over the bean mixture, then add the remaining stock. Bring to the boil, then reduce the heat and simmer for 10–15 minutes.

2 Add the red pepper, tomatoes, broad beans, and pepper to taste and simmer for a further 15–20 minutes, or until all the vegetables are tender. Stir in the chopped coriander.

3 Serve the stew topped with spoonfuls of soured cream and garnished with chopped coriander and a pinch of paprika.

Potato & Lemon Casserole

INGREDIENTS

100 ml/3½ fl oz olive oil

2 red onions, cut into 8 wedges

3 garlic cloves, crushed

2 tsp ground cumin

2 tsp ground coriander

pinch of cayenne pepper

1 carrot, thickly sliced

2 small turnips, quartered

1 courgette, sliced

500 g/1 lb 2 oz potatoes, thickly sliced

juice and grated rind of 2 large lemons

300 ml/10 fl oz vegetable stock

salt and pepper

2 tbsp chopped fresh coriander, to garnish

serves ❹

1 Heat the olive oil in a flameproof casserole. Add the onions and sauté over a medium heat, stirring frequently, for 3 minutes.

2 Add the garlic and cook for 30 seconds. Stir in the ground cumin, ground coriander and cayenne pepper and cook, stirring constantly, for 1 minute.

3 Add the carrot, turnips, courgette and potatoes and stir to coat in the oil.

4 Add the lemon juice and rind and the vegetable stock. Season to taste with salt and pepper. Cover and cook over a medium heat, stirring occasionally, for 20–30 minutes until tender.

5 Remove the lid, sprinkle in the chopped fresh coriander and stir well. Serve immediately.

Lentil & Rice Casserole

INGREDIENTS

serves **4**

225 g/8 oz red lentils

55 g/2 oz long-grain rice

1.2 litres/2 pints vegetable stock

1 leek, cut into chunks

3 garlic cloves, crushed

400 g/14 oz canned chopped tomatoes

1 tsp ground cumin

1 tsp chilli powder

1 tsp garam masala

1 red pepper, deseeded and sliced

100 g/3½ oz small broccoli florets

8 baby sweetcorn, halved lengthways

55 g/2 oz French beans, halved

1 tbsp shredded fresh basil

salt and pepper

fresh basil sprigs, to garnish

1 Place the lentils, rice and vegetable stock in a large flameproof casserole and cook over a low heat, stirring occasionally, for 20 minutes.

2 Add the leek, garlic, tomatoes and their can juices, ground cumin, chilli powder, garam masala, sliced pepper, broccoli, baby sweetcorn and French beans to the pan.

3 Bring the mixture to the boil, reduce the heat, cover and simmer for a further 10–15 minutes, or until the vegetables are tender.

4 Add the shredded basil and season to taste with salt and pepper.

5 Garnish with fresh basil sprigs and serve immediately.

Asian-Style Rice Pilau

INGREDIENTS

serves 4

1 tbsp vegetable oil

1 bunch spring onions, white and green parts, chopped

1 garlic clove, crushed

1 tsp grated fresh ginger

1 orange pepper, seeded and diced

300 g/10½ oz rice

600 ml/1 pint water

1 orange

115 g/4 oz chopped stoned dates

2 tsp sesame oil

115 g/4 oz roasted cashew nuts

2 tbsp pumpkin seeds

salt and pepper

Oriental salad vegetables, to serve

1 Heat the oil in a saucepan. Add the spring onions, garlic, ginger and pepper and cook over a medium heat, stirring frequently, for 2–3 minutes until just soft, but not brown. Add the rice and pour in the water.

2 Using a vegetable peeler, pare the rind from the orange and add the rind to the pan. Squeeze the juice from the orange into the pan. Season to taste with salt and pepper.

3 Bring to the boil, reduce the heat, cover and cook gently for 20 minutes until all the liquid has been absorbed. Remove the pan from the heat, stir in the dates and sesame oil and set aside to stand for 10 minutes.

4 Remove and discard the orange rind and stir in the cashew nuts. Pile into a warmed serving dish, sprinkle with pumpkin seeds and serve immediately with Oriental salad vegetables.

Risotto with Artichoke Hearts

INGREDIENTS

225 g/8 oz canned artichoke hearts

1 tbsp olive oil

40 g/1½ oz butter

1 small onion, finely chopped

280 g/10 oz risotto rice

1.2 litres/2 pints vegetable stock

85 g/3 oz freshly grated Parmesan or Grana Padano cheese

salt and pepper

fresh flat-leaf parsley sprigs, to garnish

serves ❹

1 Drain the artichoke hearts, reserving the liquid, and cut them into quarters.

2 Heat the oil with 25 g/1 oz of the butter in a deep saucepan over a medium heat until the butter has melted. Stir in the onion and cook gently, stirring occasionally, for 5 minutes, or until soft and starting to turn golden. Do not brown.

3 Add the rice and mix to coat in oil and butter. Cook, stirring constantly, for 2–3 minutes, or until the grains are translucent.

4 Gradually add the artichoke liquid and the hot stock, a ladle at a time. Stir constantly and add more liquid as the rice absorbs each addition. Increase the heat to medium so that the liquid bubbles. Cook for 15 minutes, then add the artichoke hearts. Cook for a further 5 minutes, or until all the liquid is absorbed and the rice is creamy. Season to taste with salt and pepper.

5 Remove the risotto from the heat and add the remaining butter. Mix well, then stir in the cheese until it melts. Season, if necessary. Spoon the risotto into warmed bowls, garnish with parsley sprigs and serve immediately.

Egg-Fried Rice with Vegetables

INGREDIENTS

2 tbsp vegetable or groundnut oil

2 garlic cloves, finely chopped

2 fresh red chillies, deseeded and chopped

115 g/4 oz mushrooms, sliced

50 g/2 oz mangetout, halved

50 g/2 oz baby sweetcorn, halved

3 tbsp Thai soy sauce

1 tbsp palm sugar or soft light brown sugar

a few Thai basil leaves

350 g/12 oz rice, cooked and cooled

2 eggs, beaten

CRISPY ONION TOPPING (OPTIONAL)

2 tbsp vegetable or groundnut oil

2 onions, sliced

serves 6–8

1 Heat the oil in a wok or large frying pan, add the garlic and chillies and fry for 2–3 minutes.

2 Add the mushrooms, mangetout and baby sweetcorn and stir-fry for 2–3 minutes before adding the soy sauce, sugar and basil. Stir in the rice.

3 Push the mixture to one side of the wok and add the eggs to the base and stir until lightly set before combining into the rice mixture.

4 If you wish to make the optional crispy onion topping, heat the oil in another frying pan and sauté the onions until crispy and brown. Serve the rice topped with the onions.

Vegetable Toad-in-the-Hole

INGREDIENTS

100 g/3½ oz plain flour

2 eggs, beaten

200 ml/7 fl oz milk

2 tbsp wholegrain mustard

2 tbsp vegetable oil

FILLING

25 g/1 oz butter

2 garlic cloves, crushed

1 onion, cut into eighths

75 g/2¾ oz baby carrots,
halved lengthways

50 g/1¾ oz French beans

50 g/1¾ oz canned
sweetcorn, drained

2 tomatoes, deseeded and
cut into chunks

1 tsp wholegrain mustard

1 tbsp chopped mixed herbs

salt and pepper

serves ❹

1 To make the batter, sift the flour and a pinch of salt into a bowl. Beat in the eggs and milk to make a batter. Stir in the mustard and leave to stand.

2 Pour the oil into a shallow ovenproof dish and heat in a preheated oven, 200°C/400°F/ Gas Mark 6, for 10 minutes.

3 To make the filling, melt the butter in a frying pan, add the garlic and onion and sauté, stirring constantly, for 2 minutes. Cook the carrots and beans in a saucepan of boiling water for 7 minutes, or until tender. Drain well.

4 Add the sweetcorn and tomatoes to the frying pan with the mustard and chopped mixed herbs. Season well and add the carrots and beans.

5 Remove the heated dish from the oven and pour in the batter. Spoon the vegetables into the centre, return to the oven and cook for 30–35 minutes, until the batter has risen and set. Serve immediately.

Aubergine Gratin

INGREDIENTS

serves ❷

4 tbsp olive oil

2 onions, finely chopped

2 garlic cloves, very finely chopped

2 aubergines, thickly sliced

3 tbsp chopped fresh flat-leaf parsley

½ tsp dried thyme

400 g/14 oz canned chopped tomatoes

175 g/6 oz mozzarella cheese, coarsely grated

6 tbsp freshly grated Parmesan cheese

salt and pepper

1 Heat the oil in a flameproof casserole over a medium heat. Add the onion and cook for 5 minutes, or until soft. Add the garlic and cook for a few seconds, or until just beginning to colour. Using a slotted spoon, transfer the onion mixture to a plate.

2 Cook the aubergine slices in batches in the same flameproof casserole until they are just lightly browned. Transfer to another plate.

3 Preheat the oven to 200°C/400°F/Gas Mark 6. Arrange a layer of aubergine slices in the base of the casserole dish or a shallow ovenproof dish. Sprinkle with some of the parsley, thyme, and salt and pepper. Add layers of onion, tomatoes and mozzarella, sprinkling parsley, thyme, salt and pepper over each layer.

4 Continue layering, finishing with a layer of aubergine slices. Sprinkle with the Parmesan cheese. Bake, uncovered, in the preheated oven for 20–30 minutes, or until the top is golden and the aubergines are tender. Serve hot.

Roast Summer Vegetables

INGREDIENTS

serves **4**

1 fennel bulb

2 red onions

2 beef tomatoes

1 aubergine

2 courgettes

1 yellow pepper, deseeded

1 red pepper, deseeded

1 orange pepper, deseeded

2 tbsp olive oil

4 garlic cloves

4 fresh rosemary sprigs

pepper

**crusty bread, to serve
(optional)**

1 Preheat the oven to 200°C/400°F/Gas Mark 6. Cut the fennel, onions and tomatoes into wedges. Thickly slice the aubergine and courgettes. Cut the peppers into chunks. Brush a large ovenproof dish with a little of the oil. Arrange the prepared vegetables in the dish and tuck the garlic cloves and rosemary sprigs among them. Drizzle with the remaining oil and season to taste with plenty of pepper.

2 Roast the vegetables in the preheated oven for 20–25 minutes, turning once, until they are tender and beginning to turn golden brown.

3 Serve the vegetables straight from the dish or transfer to a warmed serving platter. Serve immediately, with crusty bread, if using, to mop up the juices.

5 Desserts

Cooked fruit desserts lend themselves admirably to one-pot cooking – the dish can be brought straight from the oven to the table, and there are no sticky bowls or whisks to wash up. The recipes include homely favourites such as crumbles and cobblers as well as a stunning blueberry clafoutis. You'll also find recipes for a glamorous chocolate fondue, an easy-to-make one-roll pie and a bread-and-butter pudding to die for.

Apple & Blackberry Crumble

INGREDIENTS

900 g/2 lb cooking apples, peeled and sliced

300 g/10½ oz blackberries, fresh or frozen

55 g/2 oz light muscovado sugar

1 tsp ground cinnamon

single or double cream, to serve

CRUMBLE TOPPING

85 g/3 oz self-raising flour

85 g/3 oz plain wholemeal flour

115 g/4 oz unsalted butter

55 g/2 oz demerara sugar

serves ❹

1 Preheat the oven to 190°C/375°F/Gas Mark 5.

2 Peel and core the apples and cut into chunks. Place in a bowl with the blackberries, muscovado sugar and cinnamon and mix together, then transfer to an ovenproof baking dish.

3 To make the crumble topping, sift the self-raising flour into a bowl and stir in the wholemeal flour. Add the unsalted butter and rub in with your fingers until the mixture resembles fine breadcrumbs. Stir in the demerara sugar.

4 Spread the crumble over the apples and bake in the preheated oven for 40–45 minutes, or until the apples are soft and the crumble is golden brown and crisp.

5 Serve hot with cream.

Rhubarb Crumble

INGREDIENTS

900 g/2 lb rhubarb

115 g/4 oz caster sugar

**grated rind and juice of
1 orange**

**cream, yogurt or custard,
to serve**

CRUMBLE TOPPING

**225 g/8 oz plain or
wholemeal flour**

115 g/4 oz unsalted butter

115 g/4 oz soft brown sugar

1 tsp ground ginger

serves 6

1 Preheat the oven to 190°C/375°F/Gas Mark 5.

2 Cut the rhubarb into 2.5-cm/1-inch lengths and place in a 1.7-litre/3-pint ovenproof dish with the sugar and the orange rind and juice.

3 Make the crumble topping by placing the flour in a mixing bowl and rubbing in the unsalted butter until the mixture resembles breadcrumbs. Stir in the sugar and the ginger.

4 Spread the crumble evenly over the fruit and press down lightly using a fork. Bake in the centre of the oven on a baking tray for 25–30 minutes until the crumble is golden brown.

5 Serve warm with cream, yogurt or custard.

Sherried Nectarine Crumble

INGREDIENTS

6 nectarines

25 g/1 oz demerara sugar

2 tbsp sweet sherry

crème fraîche, to serve

CRUMBLE TOPPING

185 g/6½ oz plain flour

55 g/2 oz demerara sugar, plus extra for sprinkling

100 g/3½ oz unsalted butter, melted

serves ❹

1 Preheat the oven to 200°C/400°F/Gas Mark 6.

2 Using a sharp knife, halve the nectarines, remove and discard the stones, then cut the flesh into fairly thick slices. Put the nectarine slices into an ovenproof pie dish, sprinkle over the sugar and sweet sherry, and cook in the preheated oven for 5–10 minutes until heated through.

3 To make the crumble topping, put the flour and sugar in a large bowl, then quickly mix in the melted butter until crumbly. Carefully arrange the crumble over the nectarines in an even layer – keep your touch light or the crumble will sink into the filling and go mushy. Scatter a little more sugar over the top, then transfer to the preheated oven and bake for 25–30 minutes, or until the crumble topping is golden brown.

4 Serve hot with generous spoonfuls of crème fraîche.

Peach & Orange Crumble

INGREDIENTS

6 peaches

2 tbsp demerara sugar

2 tbsp orange juice

single or double cream, to serve

CRUMBLE TOPPING

115 g/4 oz self-raising flour

100 g/3½ oz unsalted butter, diced

125 g/4½ oz demerara sugar

3 tbsp finely chopped hazelnuts

serves ❹

1 Preheat the oven to 200°C/400°F/Gas Mark 6.

2 Using a sharp knife, halve the peaches, remove and discard the stones, then cut the flesh into fairly thick slices. Put the peach slices into an ovenproof pie dish, sprinkle over the sugar and orange juice, then cook in the preheated oven for 5–10 minutes until heated through.

3 To make the crumble topping, put the flour in a large bowl, then use your fingertips to rub in the unsalted butter until crumbly. Stir in 4 tablespoons of the sugar and the hazelnuts.

4 Carefully arrange the crumble over the peaches in an even layer – keep your touch light or the crumble will sink into the filling and go mushy. Scatter the remaining sugar over the top, then transfer to the preheated oven and bake for 25–30 minutes, or until the crumble topping is golden brown.

5 Serve hot with cream.

Deep Chocolate Crumble

INGREDIENTS

serves ❹

CRUMBLE TOPPING

115 g/4 oz self-raising flour

1 tbsp cocoa powder

100 g/3½ oz unsalted butter, diced

5 tbsp dark muscovado sugar

2 tbsp finely chopped pecan nuts, plus extra to decorate

50 g/1¾ oz plain chocolate, finely chopped

FILLING

60 g/2¼ oz cocoa powder

250 ml/8 fl oz water

125 g/4½ oz caster sugar

100 g/3½ oz unsalted butter, diced

4 large cooking apples

1 Preheat the oven to 180°C/350°F/Gas Mark 4.

2 To make the crumble topping, put the flour and cocoa powder in a large mixing bowl, then use your fingertips to rub in the butter until crumbly. Stir in 4 tablespoons of the sugar and the chopped pecan nuts, then stir in the chopped chocolate and set aside.

3 To make the filling, put the cocoa powder, water and caster sugar in a small saucepan and cook, stirring, over a low heat for 3 minutes. Add the diced butter and return to a simmer, stirring constantly, then remove from the heat.

4 Peel and slice the apples, then spread them evenly in the bottom of an ovenproof pie dish (this has to be done quickly to prevent the apples discolouring). Warm them through in the oven for 5–10 minutes, then pour over half of the chocolate sauce and sprinkle over the crumble topping. Scatter over the remaining sugar and bake in the preheated oven for about 20–25 minutes, or until the crumble topping is cooked.

5 Just before the end of the cooking time, return the remaining chocolate sauce to the hob and warm gently. Remove the crumble from the oven, decorate with chopped pecan nuts, and serve with the warmed chocolate sauce.

Fruit Cobbler

INGREDIENTS

900 g/2 lb fresh berries and currants, such as blackberries, blueberries, raspberries, redcurrants and blackcurrants

85–115 g/3–4 oz caster sugar

2 tbsp cornflour

single or double cream, to serve

COBBLER TOPPING

200 g/7 oz plain flour

2 tsp baking powder

pinch of salt

55 g/2 oz unsalted butter, diced and chilled

2 tbsp caster sugar

175 ml/6 fl oz buttermilk

1 tbsp demerara sugar

serves **6**

1 Preheat the oven to 200°C/400°F/Gas Mark 6.

2 Pick over the fruit, mix with the caster sugar and cornflour and put in a 25-cm/10-inch shallow, ovenproof dish.

3 To make the cobbler topping, sift the flour, baking powder and salt into a large bowl. Rub in the unsalted butter until the mixture resembles breadcrumbs, then stir in the caster sugar. Pour in the buttermilk and mix to a soft dough.

4 Drop spoonfuls of the dough on top of the fruit roughly, so that it doesn't completely cover the fruit. Sprinkle with the demerara sugar and bake in the preheated oven for 25–30 minutes until the crust is golden and the fruit is tender.

5 Remove from the oven and leave to stand for a few minutes before serving with cream.

Strawberry Cream Cobbler

INGREDIENTS

800 g/1 lb 12 oz strawberries, hulled and halved

50 g/1¾ oz caster sugar

clotted cream, to serve

COBBLER TOPPING

200 g/7 oz self-raising flour, plus extra for dusting

pinch of salt

3 tbsp butter

2 tbsp caster sugar

1 egg, beaten

25 g/1 oz sultanas

25 g/1 oz currants

about 5 tbsp milk, plus extra for glazing

serves ❹

1 Preheat the oven to 200°C/400°F/Gas Mark 6.

2 Arrange the strawberries evenly in the bottom of an ovenproof dish, then sprinkle over the sugar and cook in the preheated oven for 5–10 minutes until heated through.

3 Meanwhile, to make the cobbler topping, sift the flour and salt into a large mixing bowl. Rub in the butter until the mixture resembles fine breadcrumbs, then stir in the sugar. Add the beaten egg, then the sultanas and currants, and mix lightly until incorporated. Stir in enough of the milk to make a smooth dough. Transfer to a clean, lightly floured board, knead lightly, then roll out to a thickness of about 1 cm/½ inch. Cut out rounds using a 5-cm/2-inch biscuit cutter. Arrange the dough rounds over the strawberries, then brush the tops with a little milk.

4 Bake in the preheated oven for 25–30 minutes, or until the cobbler topping has risen and is lightly golden. Serve hot with clotted cream.

Bread & Butter Pudding

INGREDIENTS

serves 4–6

85 g/3 oz butter, softened

6 slices of thick white bread

55 g/2 oz mixed dried fruit
(sultanas, currants and
raisins)

25 g/1 oz candied peel

3 large eggs

300 ml/10 fl oz milk

150 ml/5 fl oz double cream

55 g/2 oz caster sugar

whole nutmeg, for grating

1 tbsp demerara sugar

cream, to serve

1 Preheat the oven to 180°C/350°F/Gas Mark 4.

2 Use a little of the butter to grease a 20 x 25-cm/
8 x 10-inch baking dish and butter the slices of
bread. Cut the bread into quarters and arrange
half overlapping in the dish.

3 Scatter half the dried fruit and the candied
peel over the bread, cover with the remaining
bread slices and add the remaining fruit
and peel.

4 In a mixing jug, whisk the eggs well and mix
in the milk, cream and sugar. Pour this over the
pudding and leave to stand for 15 minutes to
allow the bread to soak up some of the egg
mixture. Tuck in most of the fruit as you don't
want it to burn in the oven. Grate the nutmeg
over the top of the pudding, according to taste,
and sprinkle over the demerara sugar.

5 Place the pudding on a baking tray and bake
at the top of the oven for 30–40 minutes until
just set and golden brown.

6 Remove from the oven and serve warm with
a little pouring cream.

Bake Rice Pudding

INGREDIENTS

1 tbsp melted unsalted butter

115 g/4 oz pudding rice

55 g/2 oz caster sugar

850 ml/1½ pints milk

½ tsp vanilla extract

40 g/1½ oz unsalted butter, chilled and cut into pieces

whole nutmeg, for grating

cream, jam, fresh fruit purée, stewed fruit, honey or ice cream, to serve

serves 4–6

1 Preheat the oven to 150°C/300°F/Gas Mark 2. Grease a 1.2-litre/2-pint baking dish (a gratin dish is good) with the melted butter, place the rice in the dish and sprinkle with the sugar.

2 Heat the milk in a saucepan until almost boiling, then pour over the rice. Add the vanilla extract and stir well to dissolve the sugar.

3 Cut the butter into small pieces and scatter over the surface of the pudding.

4 Grate the whole nutmeg over the top, using as much as you like to give a good covering.

5 Place the dish on a baking tray and bake in the centre of the oven for 1½–2 hours until the pudding is well browned on the top. You can stir it after the first half hour to disperse the rice.

6 Serve hot topped with cream, jam, fresh fruit purée, stewed fruit, honey or ice cream.

Blueberry Clafoutis

INGREDIENTS

serves 4

2 tbsp butter, plus extra for greasing

125 g/4½ oz caster sugar

3 eggs

60 g/2¼ oz plain flour

250 ml/9 fl oz single cream

½ tsp ground cinnamon

450 g/1 lb blueberries

icing sugar, to decorate

single cream, to serve

1 Preheat the oven to 180°C/350°F/Gas Mark 4. Grease a 1-litre/1¾-pint ovenproof dish with butter.

2 Put the remaining butter in a bowl with the sugar and whisk together until fluffy. Add the eggs and beat together well. Mix in the flour, then gradually stir in the cream followed by the cinnamon. Continue to stir until smooth.

3 Arrange the blueberries in the bottom of the prepared dish, then pour over the cream batter. Transfer to the preheated oven and bake for about 30 minutes or until puffed and golden.

4 Remove from the oven, dust lightly with the icing sugar and serve with the cream.

One-Roll Fruit Pie

INGREDIENTS

PASTRY

85 g/3 oz butter, cut into small pieces, plus extra for greasing

175 g/6 oz plain flour

1 tbsp water

1 egg, separated

sugar lumps, crushed, for sprinkling

light or heavy cream, to serve

FILLING

600 g/1 lb 5 oz prepared plums, rhubarb or gooseberries

60 g/2¼ oz soft light brown sugar

1 tbsp ground ginger

serves ❽

1 Grease a large baking sheet with a little butter and set aside until required.

2 To make the pastry, place the butter and flour in a mixing bowl and rub in the butter with the fingertips until the mixture resembles fine breadcrumbs. Add the water and work the mixture together until a soft dough has formed. Form into a ball. Wrap the dough and chill in the refrigerator for 30 minutes.

3 Preheat the oven to 200°C/400°F/Gas Mark 6.

4 Roll out the chilled pastry to a round about 35 cm/14 inches in diameter. Transfer the pastry circle to the centre of the prepared baking sheet. Lightly beat the egg yolk, then brush the pastry with it. To make the filling, mix the plums with the sugar and ginger. Pile it into the centre of the pastry.

5 Turn in the edges of the circle of pastry all the way around. Lightly beat the egg white, then brush the surface of the pastry with it and sprinkle with the crushed sugar lumps.

6 Bake in the preheated oven for 35 minutes, or until golden brown. Serve warm with cream.

Chocolate Fondue

INGREDIENTS

1 pineapple

1 mango

12 Cape gooseberries

250 g/9 oz fresh strawberries

250 g/9 oz seedless green grapes

FONDUE

250 g/9 oz plain chocolate, broken into pieces

150 ml/5 fl oz double cream

2 tbsp brandy

serves ❻

1 Using a sharp knife, peel and core the pineapple, then cut the flesh into cubes. Peel the mango and cut the flesh into cubes. Peel back the papery outer skin of the Cape gooseberries and twist at the top to make a 'handle'. Arrange all the fruit on 6 serving plates and leave to chill in the refrigerator.

2 To make the fondue, place the chocolate and cream in a fondue pot. Heat gently, stirring constantly, until the chocolate has melted. Stir in the brandy until thoroughly blended and the chocolate mixture is smooth.

3 Place the fondue pot over the burner to keep warm. To serve, invite each guest to dip the fruit into the sauce, using fondue forks or bamboo skewers.

Index